WINNING
RETIREMENT

WINNING RETIREMENT

Proven Strategies to Make Your Money Last and to Win
Over Wall Street, Health-Care, & Big Government Spending

GREG TAYLOR

Advantage | Books

Published by Advantage Books, Charleston, South Carolina.
An imprint of Advantage Media.

ADVANTAGE is a registered trademark, and the Advantage colophon is a trademark of Advantage Media Group, Inc.

Printed in the United States of America. Second Edition.

10 9 8 7 6 5 4 3 2 1

ISBN: 979-8-89188-025-2 (Hardcover)
ISBN: 979-8-89188-026-9 (eBook)

Library of Congress Control Number: 2024907090

Cover design by Matthew Morse.
Layout design by Ruthie Wood.

This publication is designed to provide accurate and authoritative information in regard to the subject matter covered. It is sold with the understanding that the publisher is not engaged in rendering legal, accounting, or other professional services. If legal advice or other expert assistance is required, the services of a competent professional person should be sought.

Advantage Books is an imprint of Advantage Media Group. Advantage Media helps busy entrepreneurs, CEOs, and leaders write and publish a book to grow their business and become the authority in their field. Advantage authors comprise an exclusive community of industry professionals, idea-makers, and thought leaders. For more information go to **advantagemedia.com**.

To Kristin, my wife, partner, and best friend! Your belief in me and your encouragement have caused me to do more than I ever thought was possible.

To Lewis and Betty Taylor, my parents, who taught me by word and example to love God, help others, and work hard. You gave of yourselves and sacrificed to give me the opportunity to succeed.

To the hundreds of retirees I have had the privilege to coach over the past thirty-one years, you have taught me more about living life and overcoming hardships than I could ever have imagined. You have truly inspired me to have more than just a practice, to have a purpose.

CONTENTS

FOREWORD IX
BY EARLE BRUCE

INTRODUCTION 1
GAME CHANGERS

CHAPTER ONE 17
INTO A NEW SEASON

CHAPTER TWO 33
REPLACING THAT PAYCHECK

CHAPTER THREE 57
AVOIDING TAX TRAPS

CHAPTER FOUR 79
WHAT YOU LEAVE BEHIND

CHAPTER FIVE 87
IT'S ALL ABOUT TEAMWORK

CHAPTER SIX 103
HERE'S TO YOUR HEALTH

CONCLUSION 113
WINNING WAYS

ABOUT THE AUTHOR 121

IT'S A WHOLE NEW GAME 123

FOREWORD

BY EARLE BRUCE

My coaching career began in 1953 in Mansfield, Ohio, as an assistant coach at Mansfield Senior High School. In 1956, I got my first high school head coaching job at Salem High School and over four years had a record of 28-9. My twelve-year high school career ended at Massillon High School where we posted a perfect 20-0 record and won two state championships. I went on to coach college football for twenty-seven seasons and retired from college coaching with an overall record of 154-90-2. In 2002, I was honored to be inducted into the College Football Hall of Fame. At the end of my career, I told my daughters that I coached football for forty-four years but never worked a day in my life!

Throughout my career, I've experienced many incredible wins and some devastating losses. However, I was fortunate to have had a professional career that I consider a success. Some have said that winning is everything, but in football, it's the only thing. I have found that in order to be a winner—either on the football field or in life—you must do several things. You must teach discipline, build trust, assemble a quality team, demonstrate strong leadership, and develop a solid game plan. In my career, my initial goal was always to surround myself with a quality team. I tried to hire great assistant coaches, recruit talented players, and work with quality administrative personnel. A team is more than just the players on the field—everyone involved with the program can help influence success. A team that is cohesive can often achieve even more than is expected.

It takes a strong leader to set the example and promote the winning attitude. As a head coach, I needed to motivate the team, contribute to the momentum, and keep the team together after any setbacks. Some of my best games were "comebacks." It was important for me, as the head coach, to set the work ethic for the team. I worked my teams hard to build physical and mental strength, confidence, and toughness. Toughness separates great success and failure and is one trait that controls the game. If I am tougher than you, I win.

I always felt that if my teams could possess great discipline, then we could reduce the number of mistakes—penalties, fumbles, interceptions, etc.—and usually the team that makes the least mistakes wins. Instilling discipline requires strong leadership. Without leadership, a team will achieve very little. Good head coaches lead by example and lead from the front end, not the rear. In the Revolutionary War, George Washington was always riding his white horse in front of and next to his soldiers in battle.

Focusing on the basics and learning the fundamentals are critical to building a winning team. Sometimes, you must take your weakest link and give it more focus. If one of your fundamentals, such as tackling for instance, is suffering, you must make it your priority. Drill, drill, drill and then when you see a great tackle, you must point out its value to the success of the game and be sure to make it a teaching moment for your players.

If I were a coach today, I would give the same advice that I received when I was a young coach: win all your home games, place special emphasis on your arch rivalries, and when you're challenged by a great team on your home turf, turn to the discipline you've followed, fundamentals you've learned, and toughness you've built, and go out and win the game!

Just like in football, successful retirement planning requires learning the fundamentals, demonstrating discipline, building trust, partnering with a strong leader, and, yes, showing toughness to help get you through the ups and downs. When I was young, there was no need for a financial planner because we had very little money left from our paycheck to save. When I moved into college coaching and made a little more money, planning was still pretty easy—this was when interest on a Certificate of Deposit (CD) was 20–25 percent, and we saw tremendous growth in our funds. After things started going south and I heard a lot of "just hang in there and it'll get better," I realized that a retirement planner—or head coach—would help build a successful financial future. A great retirement "game plan" can provide all the tools for success, and a quality financial planner can help you realize a comfortable retirement ensuring your money will last.

Reading Greg Taylor's *Winning Retirement* will teach you the discipline and financial fundamentals required to help make your money last during retirement. He has taught me many strategies to make a difference in my retirement, and I'm certain that the strategies you will learn in this book will make a difference in yours. Trust Greg Taylor to become your partner in retirement planning and help you build a foundation. He provides practical financial advice and winning strategies to avoid mistakes and ensure a quality and successful retirement season.

"Three things can happen when you throw the ball, and two of them are bad."
—Woody Hayes

INTRODUCTION

GAME CHANGERS

I grew up watching the Cleveland Browns. The Colts were always my favorite team, but central Ohio rooted for the Browns. In 1988, the Browns finally had a shot to get to the Super Bowl. They were in the AFC Championship Game against the Broncos at Denver's Mile High Stadium, and hopes were high as the team battled its way up from 21-3 at halftime. Right at the goal line, the ball was handed off to running back Earnest Byner, and it looked as if he was going to strut in for a game-tying touchdown with moments to spare. But just before he crossed the goal line, the ball was stripped from his hands. The Browns didn't make it to the Super Bowl, and people here still feel the pain. Byner was one of the main reasons Cleveland came so close to victory—but fans and the media focused on his lapse at the critical moment. The fateful play is known to this day as "the Fumble."

A game changer, most certainly. When it looks as if you've won the game, that's what can happen. And it's a lesson for those who are headed down the field to their retirement or already have made it to the end zone. You can think you have a wonderful retirement in store, but something goes wrong—the market declines, you or your spouse take ill, you're blindsided by taxes—and because you haven't planned for it, you fumble your retirement.

Last-minute mistakes—or strategy lapses made much earlier in your season—truly can lead you and your loved ones to great pain, financially and emotionally.

Freedom from Worry

I'm here to tell you that it need not be that way. This book is for people who want to be prepared as they approach their retirement. My goal is to help those who have worked hard, saved their money, and don't want to worry in retirement about whether they will have enough money to last the rest of their lives.

All around us these days are the "millionaires next door"—those who have saved their first million through hard work and thrift, or are approaching that goal, and perhaps have far exceeded it. You wouldn't recognize the millionaires next door. One of my clients made millions on UPS stock. He drives an older model Cadillac that he bought used. He comes into the office wearing a flannel shirt, bib overalls, and a Buckeyes hat, talking about his hunting trips to Michigan. He's not the sort of paunchy millionaire you see pictured on the Monopoly board with the tux and top hat. Another client wears blue jeans and a sweater vest but has a million in his 401(k). We worked on setting up an income plan to keep him and his wife living well for the rest of their lives.

Millionaires or not, retirees have this in common: They're worried about having enough to last. They're worried about keeping pace with inflation. They likely expect to live a long time, and chances are, they will. If two people live past the age of sixty-five, there's about a 73 percent chance that one of them is going to live to ninety-three.

This book will offer some practical advice that retirees, or those soon to join those ranks, badly need at this stage in their lives.

Many have heard the same line from their brokers: "We're going to put you in some bonds, and some growth mutual funds, and some mid-cap and some small-cap—and we think that you're going to be able to withdraw about 4 percent of your money each year and it should last till you're ninety-five." And then, when the markets tanked, they heard another refrain: "Hang in there. It should come back eventually."

Now, imagine you have taken your seat in a jetliner and the pilot announces, "Welcome aboard, folks, and buckle your belts for takeoff. We're seeing some rough weather between here and your destination, but we'll make it there eventually. Or at least we should. Don't you worry. I'm an expert pilot, and my computer calculations show a 90 percent chance we'll get there safely."

You'd be out of your seat and headed for the door, posthaste. Why? Because it's a matter of life or death. And financial well-being feels like life and death to retirees when they have so much at stake. If Mr. Jones is given a 90 percent chance that his money will last the rest of his life, will he be resting in peace when his ninety-two-year-old widow learns the money is gone?

Whether you are that millionaire next door or a person of more modest means, this book can help you make the most of your assets.

Starting with the Foundation

When you build a house, where do you begin? With the foundation. You can build a gorgeous house that's level and plumb, but without a good foundation, it soon will be a shambles. So, what is the foundation of a good retirement plan? It's knowing that your income will never run out. If you don't have enough income, you can't live the way you want to live.

After you get a good foundation in place, you start work on the walls and the roof. In your financial house, the walls would be the equivalent of growth investments that you need to keep up with inflation and the prospect of living to age one hundred. You need to have an element of growth, but that growth needs to be well managed. It needs to be watched over in a way that most managers aren't doing.

The roof of your financial house includes a solid insurance plan—a home policy, an auto policy, health insurance, a long-term care strategy—as well as estate planning, so that whatever remains of your assets when you are gone will pass efficiently to your loved ones, not the tax man. Like the roof of your house, comprehensive planning has got you covered.

You need to consider every facet of your retirement planning, and it needs to make sense for you. I might find myself in my conference room, meeting with prospective clients on their retirement income plans, while down the hall in another conference room, our estate planning attorney is meeting with other clients, and in another room, our insurance expert is determining whether a client is paying a reasonable amount for auto and home and medical coverages and whether an umbrella policy would be appropriate. We need to get all the bases covered. That's why retirement embodies a team concept. No one person knows enough to do everything.

Game Changers and Eye Openers

"Greg, everything was going good until age fifty-six," a potential client recently told me. "I went to the gym one morning, ran three miles and worked out for two hours, and came home and had a heart attack."

"That was a game changer for me," he said. "I realized I needed to change the way I eat. I needed to change the way I look at life. I needed to change the way I treat my family."

"My eyes were opened. I realized that things don't last forever, that I have to live my life on purpose. I can't just let it go by each day."

As we travel through life, we reach milestones and crisis points that redefine and redirect us and change our perspective. These are the game changers that come to each and every one of us. High school graduation is a game changer. So is graduating from college. Getting married, having children, buying your first home. Getting into debt and out of debt. Facing an unforeseen health need. Divorce, or the death of a spouse. Those are all game changers.

Getting older is itself a game changer, as is holding your first grandchild—and entering retirement. Game changers can be things that happen to you, but they can also be things that you can exert control over. You will get older inevitably, but you can certainly influence the quality of your retirement years.

It would be sad to look back and realize you could have done better but didn't. "I could have been a better husband, but I wasn't. I could have been a better dad, but I wasn't. I could have been a better worker, but I wasn't. I could have done more. I could have done my best, but I chose to do less." We sometimes look back with regrets about how we played the game.

A New Season of Life

During your working years, you strive to put money aside. You invest your savings, and if the markets fall, you tend not to worry because you're not withdrawing those savings—in fact, you're buying your investments at a discount. You're saving for the future.

But when you retire, the future has arrived. You may need that money as income. You need it to live day by day, so you may have to withdraw it. And if that money is still invested in the rising and falling markets, your retirement is at risk. It's difficult if not impossible to recover your wealth when you are withdrawing money from accounts invested in a bear market. If things don't go your way, your nest egg can be devastated in just a few years.

In retirement, you are in a new season of life. You have a lot more time on your hands—and what are you going to do with it? Will you have enough money to do what you truly want to do? For one person, the game changer of retirement will mean playing golf several times a week, and that's a thrill. Others welcome the opportunity to donate time to a favorite cause. Many will be delighted to spend more time with their children and grandchildren. Or they simply anticipate relaxing and not feeling the stress of that demanding job.

> Retirement can be a beautiful and rewarding time of life, but it can be a frightening one.

Retirement can be a beautiful and rewarding time of life, but it can be a frightening one. You are moving into a different financial phase of life as well—one in which your income, for better or worse, is fixed. You might get some cost-of-living increases along the way, but those typically are too modest to keep pace with the demands of life and the economy. The nest egg you have nurtured during your working years must now last you for the rest of your life—and you must protect it.

Defensive Strategies

On New Year's Eve in 2022, our beloved Ohio State Buckeyes were in the semifinal game against the Georgia Bulldogs. The Buckeyes were ahead by two touchdowns going into the fourth quarter in that game, but even though we had one of the more lethal offenses in the country, our defense found a way to let us down.

A winning portfolio needs to have both offense and defense. The offense is your growth over time, and you must realize that you will likely need to take some risks to accomplish your goals. But if you get overconfident in your offense, oftentimes that can wreak havoc on your defense. The defense is there for your protection.

When it comes to retirement, you need to know you have a strong defense on your side—one that will keep you from getting wiped out in the heat of the game. You need a winning strategy.

In short, you need to make sure that what you have accumulated all your life is not taken away by somebody else. If life's events, a pandemic, politicians, or some other world event should once again shake the confidence of the markets, you don't want your portfolio to suffer. You don't want what happens in Russia, Ukraine, Greece, Japan, China, or any other country to hurt your account. You don't want the government's out-of-control spending to diminish your retirement account. You need to be in control.

You have to have a defensive strategy in place because one of three things can happen. The market can be bullish. The market can stay stagnant over a sustained period of time—what's called a sideways market. Or the market can be a bear. Only one of those will allow you to have a winning retirement. Unless you have a good defense, the other two will cause you to fail. As Woody Hayes, the great coach of the Buckeyes, said, "Three things can happen when you throw the ball, and two of them are bad."

Your defensive strategy includes keeping your money away from Uncle Sam. That 401(k) or IRA that you have built so faithfully for years could become a tax trap. Same with your 403(b) or your deferred compensation. Each essentially involves a loan from the government—and one in which the terms of repayment are left ambiguous. Uncle Sam controls the amount we have to withdraw, and when, and how much he will charge us when we do. We have been misled into believing that we will one day withdraw our savings in a lower tax bracket. But the tax rate is historically low right now. It's likely that retirement plan investors will face a higher bracket.

Another issue that calls for a good defensive strategy is probate. Probate is a legal word meaning the process of proving your will to be true and valid. So, what does that mean? That means that if you have a will, your estate will go through probate. And if you don't have a will, your estate will go through probate. It's guaranteed—and also guaranteed to take longer. The length of time it generally takes to settle an estate through probate is anywhere from nine months to two years. John Wayne's estate went through probate for several years, and it only ended when it ran out of money.

There are more effective strategies, as we will discuss, to protect your estate—and your peace of mind.

When the Paychecks Stop

A lot of people approach retirement thinking everything's going to fall into place. But that's like thinking you can dump a jigsaw puzzle out of the box and it will magically assemble itself. It just doesn't happen. You have to have a plan. My job is to help families create that plan. "Let's get to the point," I tell them, "where we know that your entire financial house is in order, and that it's going to stay that way for the rest of your life."

You know that adage "plan your work and work your plan"? In meeting with a client, I'll draw lines on my whiteboard connecting various aspects of his or her financial planning needs—IRA account, savings account, checking account, certificates of deposit (CDs), insurance policy, long-term care insurance, this thing, that thing. "Now, what's your plan?" I ask. "You've got a bunch of stuff. What's your plan?" And that's where we begin, because very often the client just doesn't know.

That's the same awakening that retirees often face after they get their last paycheck. They vaguely believe they'll have money coming in for the rest of their lives—but how will that happen? What structure is in place to guarantee an income that won't cease?

I don't know it all, nor can I do it all. I function as an advisor. I am personally hands-on as the fiduciary advisor, but I realize that I have a limitation on time, so I have an entire team of portfolio managers that I lean on to help manage the assets for our clients. They are fiduciaries as well. We also have strategic partnerships with estate planning and elder law attorneys; we have long-time relationships with insurance professionals to help with Medicare questions; and we work with certified public accountants (CPAs) and other tax profes-sionals. We have a team around us, people who are well-experienced in estate planning, insurance, and elder law so that nothing slips through the cracks in your plan.

Most people are smart enough to know when they don't know. If you dump a puzzle on the floor, you're smart enough to pick up those pieces and start assembling them into a picture, but it takes time and dedication to use your smarts. And it's not necessarily your own smarts. Most people who have had successful careers understand how to delegate. They're familiar with surrounding themselves with reliable advisors.

A financial advisor who has your best interests at heart can help you avoid pitfalls in your plan, like the heartbreaking one a radio listener experienced a few years ago. After hearing us on the radio show, a lady came to us asking for help. She and her husband had both been very successful. He had been a high-level executive and had a rather large pension. But that pension would be significantly reduced if he made his wife a beneficiary on it. A life insurance salesman had convinced him to do a pension maximation and then buy a life insurance policy with his wife as beneficiary. That maximization would allow him to take a full pension, and the insurance policy would take care of his wife.

> Thinking your retirement will just fall into place is like dumping a jigsaw puzzle on the floor and hoping it will assemble itself.

The husband agreed and took out a single-life annuity on his pension and then applied for the life insurance policy. As part of the life insurance application, he was required to undergo a physical examination—that's when he found out he had cancer. A little over a year later, he passed away and his wife was left with only around $750,000 that they had saved from his 401(k). She took that money to a broker, who put it all in the stock market. It went through the 2008 recession, and the 2018 drop, and the 2020 pandemic drop. By the time she came to visit us, she had just under $100,000 left and she needed $25,000 a year to live on.

At that point, there wasn't really much we could do to help this dear lady—I felt so helpless, and my wife, Kristin, and I cried with her in the conference room as she told us her story. Unfortunately, the reality is when you're out of money, you're out of options. I'm sure the life insurance salesman meant well, but his job was to sell life insurance. I'm sure the broker meant well, but the broker's job is to put money in stocks, bonds, and mutual funds. It's not that those tools are necessarily bad tools; it's just that, before a pension option was ever decided, there should have already been an approved policy in place. And before money was put at risk in the stock market, the income this dear lady needed for retirement should have been secured.

Protecting your retirement paycheck is crucial. You must be confident about your financial future—or as I often say, you must know that you don't know everything. You must be certain where that paycheck is coming from. And for couples facing the future together, consider this: What happens if one of you dies? Typically, income drops 30–50 percent. Are you prepared to replace that source?

When it comes to your retirement planning, make sure you are working with a fiduciary who is obligated to do what is in your best interest. Brokers sell a lot of annuities, with fees that range from 3 to 5 percent. If someone told you upfront that you were going to pay 3–5 percent inside of such an account, you might think twice before buying it—that's not uncommon for most people. What if you could have an account that brought higher income with lower fees? Wouldn't that be more along the lines of what is in your best interest? When my team and I put together income plans, and we're considering annuities as part of that plan, we look for those kinds of products—the ones that require the absolute least amount of money into the account to accomplish an income goal. We've come up with a lot of creative strategies to maximize the income for the least amount of money, so that there is more money left over for growth. That's how a fiduciary looks for ways to do what is in your best interest.

My job as a fiduciary is to make sure I'm doing what's best for you; I'm legally obligated to act in my clients' best interest, but I also do so because I have a pastor's heart.

When Our Bodies Wear Out

In 1986, I was an assistant pastor at Calvary Baptist Church in Memphis, Tennessee. Three doors down from me lived a man named Mr. Flynn. Mr. Flynn had worked for forty-seven years as a mechanic for a Buick dealership in Memphis. He had saved over $600,000 working hourly.

When I met Mr. Flynn, he had been retired for eight years, and for six of those years, he had been visiting his wife every day in a nursing home. In those days, there were far fewer healthcare facilities. Very few people had long-term care insurance or had even heard of it. You could tell Mr. Flynn had burdens, but he was friendly and would stop to chat while mowing the grass.

Three years later, Mr. Flynn's nest egg was down to just over $70,000. That's all he had left. The only time I would see him outside was when he'd shuffle out to his mailbox and back, his body slumped. He seemed totally defeated.

It's a sad image, but true, and it raises the question: Are we destined to do our best and save our money and invest it well and keep it safe, just to have it stripped away from us by healthcare costs?

Let me tell you a happier story. Some few years ago, I met Jack LaLanne, the long-time guru of physical fitness. He was ninety when I met him, and he and his wife Elaine were still exercising at the gym for one hour every day. He was very active and health conscious. On his seventieth birthday, he swam for a mile with his hands and feet shackled and a harness around his waist tied to a string of seventy rowboats, each with a man in it. He pulled those seventy rowboats a mile. Twenty years later, he was still vigorous—and one of the most delightful retirees I have ever met.

It's so important to take care of your health, to stay active, and to eat right. Taking care of yourself can add many active years to your retirement. But even so, Father Time catches up. Are you prepared? There is much you can do to be ready, if and when healthcare issues arise.

Some people have chosen to purchase long-term care insurance and that can be a good option. I give them some tips as to what to look for in a good policy. A 2021 study by Genworth Financial, "Genworth 2021 Cost of Care Survey Ohio," determined that in Columbus, Ohio, the average cost is $283 per day. According to AARP and the *New England Journal of Medicine*, around 72 percent of married couples who live past the age of sixty-five will receive some kind of long-term care while they're alive. The average length of that is about two and a half years. In Franklin County, Ohio, the average cost is $260 per day. And if you are single, there's about a 51 percent chance that you are going to need care.

Some people, to save on premiums, are willing to play the odds and bet that they won't need long-term care. But what if there's a way to hedge that bet and win either way? What if you could pay into a program that would provide for your care if you needed it, but otherwise would make a payout to your family, tax-free, when you died? It's possible, and I will explain how in this book.

You Need a Coach

When people come in to meet with me, they have a lot of documents and accounts. They might have life insurance and long-term care insurance, a will, power of attorney. They have money in the bank, in a 401(k), or in a brokerage. They have all these elements, but they're trying to decide, "Okay, do I have enough? Have I done enough? Am I going to make it through my retirement?" And they don't know.

If they're worried about what has happened in the markets, their guy on Wall Street will say, "Just hang in there. It'll get better. The market always comes back." That's the standard line. The broker will explain that the market has rebounded in the past, and he may even show a performance chart of the last thirty years. "You should be able to pull out 4 percent a year from your investments for retirement income," the broker may say, "and there's a good chance you'll never run out."

What they really need is someone to put all those pieces together and say, "Okay. Let's take a close look. Let's look at the legal areas and make sure you have the right expert guiding you. Let's make sure you're not paying too much in taxes; you need good tax planning, not just preparation. Let's make sure you have long-term care protection, not just a long-term care policy." We put all the pieces together like a puzzle so they can see a clear picture.

That, to me, is what coaching is. It's saying, "Okay, here's where you are, and there's where you want to go. Let's consider how you're going to reach your goal." It's similar to the role of an athletic coach. The players are very much able. They have the skills. They know how to handle the ball, but they sure can't win unless they have a game plan.

As a financial coach, I create a game plan for making it through retirement. I work with a team of other professionals, in the way a football team might have a wide receivers' coach, an offensive and defensive line coach, and a quarterback coach.

Good coaching ensures everything is in place for the win. It anticipates the curve balls we all face, those game-changing moments. Retirement coaching isn't just about telling people where to put their money. It's showing them how they're going to succeed through retirement. Like a sports coach, the retirement coach strives to instill a sense of confidence when times seem confusing.

"What makes the difference," said the eminently quotable Coach Bear Bryant, "isn't the will to win but the willingness to prepare." Everybody wants to succeed. Even a guy who's too lazy to get off the couch would like to be seen as a success. But those who get the opportunities for success are those who put a plan in motion. They get set to go.

"What you plant now, you will harvest later."
—Og Mandino

CHAPTER ONE

INTO A NEW SEASON

When you are young and just starting out, you are concerned about keeping your head above water. You're concerned about whether you'll have enough money to buy gas and groceries and balance a modest budget. As a young couple, you finally get to a place where you are able to save for a down payment and buy that first home. Then, along come children, and you want to set aside money for their college educations and to get them launched. Meanwhile, you strive to advance in your career.

Then, one day, a light comes on. It occurs to you that one day you may not be able to work, or may not want to work, or your employer might not let you work.

"I'd better be prepared," you say to yourself. "I'm going to start setting some money aside." So, you put money into an IRA or a 401(k) or a brokerage account. You invest in stocks and mutual funds, and you figure it will work out. Or, if you're really conservative, you squirrel away savings in a bank.

You don't intend to touch that money for years to come; growth is the primary objective for those savings during your working years.

You are looking to the future, and you're not as concerned about keeping up with the Joneses as you are about making sure that you're able to keep up for yourself.

Inflation raises your cost of living during those working years, and taxes may rise, but you don't worry much about it because you get regular raises, so your paycheck keeps pace. That's why you're working so hard—to keep a good job that gives you those raises and provides you an income that is sufficient for more than your immediate needs.

You proceed for years, and decades, on that track. You are advancing, saving, dreaming of what you will do someday. And then, you turn the corner into retirement. It is time to realize those dreams.

Fear of the Unknown

All of your adult life you have had that paycheck coming in. Now, in retirement, you're responsible for your own paycheck. Maybe you're counting on Social Security and its continued funding. Perhaps you're fortunate enough to have a pension—as might be the case if you are a state retiree, or if you were a teacher, or if you worked for one of those rare few companies that still offer them. But your Social Security benefit and those pensions typically aren't going to be close to what you earned while working. They certainly don't adequately keep pace with inflation.

> All of your adult life you have had that paycheck coming in. Now, in retirement, you're responsible for your own paycheck.

You may feel you have to make a tough decision: Should you subject your life's savings to market risk in hopes of making enough to sustain your lifestyle, or should you lower your standard of living? You may be uncertain whether you need to do either.

In retirement, you now have time on your hands, and hopefully good health—but you're not sure if you have enough money to last throughout retirement.

I recently met with a couple who paid $100,000 for a large travel trailer. They had long wanted to see the country, and retirement had brought them the opportunity. "That's a beauty," I told them.

"Tell me about the trips you have planned this year." They looked at each other—and then the wife told me that her husband was worried about the cost of gas.

I smiled at him and couldn't resist a little teasing. "So, hmm, you paid all that money to travel in style, and you're worried about the price of gas?" He tried to explain, but I pointed out that gas prices would rise and fall but they couldn't pin their dreams on that. "If you're going to travel," I suggested, "now's the time."

Such concerns are common among retirees. They want to pursue their goals, but the unknown haunts them. They may believe rationally that their assets should be sufficient, but they just can't feel confident. If their money is in stocks and other risky investments, they fear that the market might do to them what they have seen it do to other retirees' nest eggs. They're concerned that something will happen—the economy will fizzle, or their health will fail—and their money won't last.

Many retirees are longing for security, and yet, they are still investing as they did during their working years, when they could take risks in hopes of a higher return. When they were trying to accumulate enough wealth to provide peace of mind in retirement, peace of mind is key and that begins by talking about the things that are most bothersome, so we can address them in advance. Everyone's concerns are different because of their own life experiences. For instance, if both parents went to a nursing home, then a person might be very concerned about long-term care. But in retirement, our focus shifts from accumulation to now having to take distributions. We need to consider more than just the accumulation of wealth. We now need to consider the ability to take consistent distributions over our lifetime.

Protecting Your Nest Egg

It's not uncommon for retirees to lose much of the assets they garnered in a lifetime because they manage their finances unwisely. It comes down to this: if you are drawing income from an account that fluctuates with market investments, you are at risk of seeing your nest egg vanish. Wise financial management in retirement, as we shall see, requires that you know where your income is coming from and that it will derive from the three worlds of money: banks and credit unions, insurance, and Wall Street brokerage firms.

Each of the three worlds of money comes with a string attached. Banks and credit unions offer checking and savings accounts, money market accounts, and CDs; these assets are safe and liquid, but they don't keep pace with inflation. Insurance companies offer life insurance and annuities; these have growth potential and can provide a dependable stream of income, but they are not 100 percent liquid. Then, there is the brokerage world, which offers stocks, bonds, mutual funds, exchange-traded funds, commodities, and alternative investments. These products have the most growth potential and are, for the most part, liquid, but the string attached is that you can lose your money. There's always a string attached; you just need to make sure you understand what that string is and how it fits into your overall retirement plan.

Your overall retirement plan is about having your financial house in order and keeping it that way. You need to protect your investments from loss. Yes, you need a reasonable return, but you want to protect your money from taking a big hit, because when you are of retirement age, you simply won't have time to recover. It's time to shift your investment focus from the accumulation stage of your working years into the distribution phase of your retirement years. In this phase, it's more important than ever to be efficient.

Your nest egg faces other threats. You also must consider the slow erosion of inflation. If you were to put all your money in a bank CD paying a low rate of interest, you would see the value of your assets slip away as the cost of living outpaced your earnings. The cost of healthcare also can deal a severe blow to your finances. You could face the need to spend dearly for nursing care or a variety of expensive medications. I have clients who spend over $1,000 a month on their medications.

Besides the risks of a volatile market, inflation, and healthcare needs, you may face another threat to your nest egg: a drain from children and family members whom you are trying to help. I have many clients right now whose children, through unfortunate events in life (or divorce, or the poor job market, or sheer laziness), are leaning more and more on Mom and Dad. It's an unfortunate situation: in retirement, you don't want to be worrying about your adult children.

On the flip side, some retirees also are concerned about preserving their money, so they will have a surplus and can leave a sizable bequest to their children and heirs. They want to know that all their life's hard work has amounted to more than just surviving retirement. This is a prime concern for perhaps a third of retirees, although a few could care less whether their children and heirs get anything. Most people, however, want to leave something—they would rather their children get the money than the government. And they are concerned about what their children will do with that inheritance: they want to distribute it equitably, but they know one child likely would manage money maturely while another would blow it. What's the best way to deal with that?

These are universal concerns among retirees as they assess their situation. They want to maintain the lifestyle to which they have become accustomed, but they want to make sure they don't go broke before they die. They want to make sure they have enough liquid assets available for emergencies and other contingencies—whether it's a family crisis or the roof needs to be replaced.

All those worries could easily keep you awake at night, and part of what I do is provide sleep insurance. I help people rest easy, knowing that they have their affairs in order. They can see that their money will last their lifetime and exactly how that will be so. They know that they no longer need to worry.

> These are universal concerns among retirees. They want to maintain their lifestyle, but they don't want to go broke before they die.

That's what retirement is all about. You should be able to enjoy yourself. You have worked hard for many years. Why spend what could be the most joyous time of your life fretting about things that might not be as big a problem as you think they are?

What you need is good coaching so that sense of confidence can be instilled in you. You can move forward knowing that your income will be sufficient to support your lifestyle for the rest of your days.

Today, Tomorrow, Forever

When we're creating a retirement plan that involves the three worlds of money—banks and credit unions, insurance, and Wall Street brokerage firms—we look at having three kinds of money in place. First, there is the "today" money, which is your income; this is money that lets you live your retirement life. It's your lifestyle money, the money you need to pay your bills, go on vacation, or do something special with the grandkids. Then, there is "tomorrow" money, which is liquid assets available for unexpected needs, major purchases, or emergencies. Liquid money lets you sleep well at night. Once you have income for your lifestyle and money in the bank for emergencies, then you need your "forever" money, which is money that you can afford to take risks with. Forever money is your growth money; it's to help with future inflation, tax increases, and healthcare costs. Growth money is money that you never want to deplete by spending down the principal. You don't ever want to use up that principal because it provides the earnings to replenish the first two.

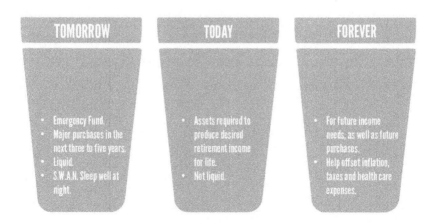

YOUR RETIREMENT PORTFOLIO

THREE BUCKETS

TOMORROW
- Emergency Fund.
- Major purchases in the next three to five years.
- Liquid.
- S.W.A.N. Sleep well at night.

TODAY
- Assets required to produce desired retirement income for life.
- Not liquid.

FOREVER
- For future income needs, as well as future purchases.
- Help offset inflation, taxes and health care expenses.

I often refer to these three kinds of money as buckets. You need all three buckets in your retirement plan, and there needs to be balance. Like eating a balanced diet of vegetables, fruits, and protein to sustain our health, we need liquidity, income, and growth to sustain our financial health.

Having one type of bucket isn't sufficient because you need your money to do different things. You need liquid money to live on today; you need money for tomorrow for the unknowns. If you only have liquidity, you're going to lose pace with inflation. If you only have income, what are you going to do later on for growth? If you only have growth, how do you deal with all the risk—what is the risk, is it consistent?

And you need forever money that you don't outlive. That's what gives you peace of mind and security when entering or in retirement. You want to know your advisor has a plan for you and cares about what happens in your life and wants you to have money to pay your bills today, and to do the things that you've always promised yourself that you would do.

The trouble with our industry is that those who only sell stocks, bonds, and mutual funds think you need to put all your money in those vehicles and they try to scare you from putting your money anywhere else. They tell you annuities are bad because they don't sell them or they sell the terrible kind that requires you to pay 3–5 percent in fees. Then, there's the insurance agent, who tries to scare you away from the stock market, or the banker who wants you to keep all of your money in their bank.

Well, the truth is none of that is right. You need a balance of all three buckets for the best financial health in retirement.

When I sit down with a client to create a retirement plan, we first need to define the goals for today, tomorrow, and forever so we know how much money will be required to fulfill them. I sit down for an hour and a half and listen to people tell me about their goals. I want to know what's important to them, because our plan is going to focus on that. If I know someone wants to buy a piece of property, then I know they have to have more liquidity. Others have few major plans; they just want to live day by day, without fancy vacations or big purchases. They find peace of mind in living frugally so that they are more likely to never run out of money.

Older retirees in their eighties and nineties tend to be more conservative because they are more likely to have experienced the effects of the Great Depression early in life. They tend to be more concerned about leaving legacies to their kids than younger retirees are, born during the World War II years or its baby boom aftermath. Those whose attitudes toward money were formed in the roaring postwar years tend to be more willing to spend.

But whatever their mindset, when we begin talking about dreams and goals, I find that new retirees often are less than articulate about what they want for the rest of their lives and how they want to be remembered. Most simply say they just don't want to run out of money. With a little questioning, I'm able to draw them out.

"Share with me a goal that you might have," I say, "that would take both money and planning to achieve. What would that be for you?" Almost every time, the first reaction is along the lines of this: "I just don't ever want to run out of money." So, I drill down to find out what motivates them. "Are you charitably minded?" I ask if they are interested in giving money to charity or if they would like to leave something behind for their grandchildren.

Eventually, I get them to open up about what's truly important to them. For some, it's being able to help out their loved ones while they're living. They want to give of themselves while they're alive, so

25

they can see the expression on the face of their grandchild or their son or daughter. They want to enjoy life and share their money, whether with charities or their family. That's what is truly important to them.

> Whether you have enough money depends on your dreams and goals and what life has dealt you.

I learn from others that health challenges have compromised their goals and dreams. I have a client who had been anticipating retirement with his wife but was in a car accident that left him a paraplegic. He gets around in a cart that he can operate with his hands, but suddenly all their retirement plans—the traveling, the golf—are gone. Now, they just want to survive.

Those words "I never want to run out of money" are relative, because whether you have enough money depends on your dreams and goals and what life has dealt you.

We Do the Math

When it comes to the parts of a plan, there are your goals, the principles that are guiding your retirement financial plan, and then the fundamental shift from the accumulation to distribution phase. If, in 2000, you had $1 million, it would grow over the last twenty-plus years. In fact, over that time, it would have averaged almost 10 percent per year just being in the S&P 500. However, if you were pulling out 4 percent per year, even if you were averaging nearly 10 percent growth, your portfolio would be down around 40 percent over that period of time. How can you average 10 percent, pull out 4 percent, and still lose money? It's called sequence of returns risk. You don't notice it when you're putting money in, but you do notice it when you're taking money out. Later in the book, I'll talk more about this.

The bottom line falls back on the adage: "If it ain't broke, don't fix it." We are so used to investing in the stock market for growth, but we do not realize that the ups and downs of the market react differently to withdrawals than it does to accumulation. The vehicles we use to accumulate our wealth may not be the best vehicles to take distributions when we want security in retirement.

We walk clients through a process using a tool called "My Retirement Kit." As part of that process, we want to understand someone's true needs and wants. In that first appointment with clients, we're interviewing potential clients to better understand them, and they're interviewing us to see if we're the people they can trust and whether we can actually help. Part of that process is understanding the true income need, not just expenses but also lifestyle. Often, they'll tell us they only need $30,000 or $40,000 a year in retirement.

But as we dig deeper, we find they are just considering their predictable expenses, not their lifestyle. Maybe they're currently working and making $90,000 per year and that $30,000 to $40,000 is their expenses. It's not taking into consideration new tires on the car or random trips to Target to pick up two items but then putting $200 on the credit card. How do we solve for that gap? Then, we look at income—Social Security, maybe a small pension, some savings. Together, those might equal $50,000 per year; that leaves a gap of $40,000. But we have to also consider things like taxes of, say, $20,000, which makes the gap $60,000. Filling that gap might take $1.2 million. If the person has only saved $500,000, then I have to ask: "Are you willing to change the way you're used to living? Or would you prefer to work a little longer and save a little more?"

Sometimes, that conversation is a reality check; sometimes, it's permission to retire. It's all based on how things go when we run the numbers. We love to do the math because I'm not going to tell someone that they're okay just to get them to become a client and then later pull the rug out from under them by telling them, "Just kidding. You can't really retire now." It's just unfair to give families unrealistic expectations.

Don't feel that you are alone, however, in worrying whether you can stretch your life's savings to last throughout your retirement. These are age-old concerns that older people have been feeling for generations. Once you look at the figures, you well may see that you're going to be in better shape than you thought you would be.

You need a financial advisor to partner with you to help you see the light at the end of the tunnel. A retirement advisor works specifically with people transitioning into retirement or who are already retired and are focusing solely on that phase of their financial life. They understand that the tools and philosophies of the accumulation and distribution phases are different; that in the distribution phase, Social Security and Medicare are also a big part of the transition; and that now, more than ever, it is vitally important for retirees to have their own written retirement income plan.

A World of Change

Recently, a very sharp lady who had a role high up in one of the local banks called me. She had done a great job of saving a couple of million dollars. The bank was giving her a buyout. Someone else who worked at the bank told her not to take her Social Security yet but to instead wait for full retirement age. She was only sixty-four at the time, so I asked her if she really understood the pros and cons of waiting. She understood that waiting meant she would get an additional 8 percent more per year and that kind of return would be difficult to find anywhere else. So, I sat down with her and we looked at the math.

By not claiming yet, she would not be receiving $2,500 per month from Social Security; for the next three years, she would not receive $30,000 per year or $90,000 total. That also meant that she would have to spend $90,000 of her own money—technically, it would cost her $180,000, but it would give her $700 more per month to wait three years. Doing the math—dividing $180,000 by $700 equals 257 months; divide that by twelve (months in a year) equals twenty-one years. In other words, she would break even at age eighty-eight, assuming that the $90,000 of her own money didn't grow over that twenty-one years.

While the person who advised her was only focused on the 8 percent, I've spent dozens of hours researching this and what I've learned is that Social Security calculators only calculate the benefit you don't receive, they don't calculate what you spend of your own cash. That 8 percent doesn't really look that appealing if, at worst, you make nothing on your money and you have to be eighty-eight years old to break even. After she saw the math, she said, "I'm going to apply for Social Security right away."

When the Social Security system was inaugurated, this country had many more workers than retirees. Today, as the baby boomer generation ages into retirement, we have more and more retirees—and relatively fewer workers whose paycheck deductions support them. Complicating the situation is the dramatic increase in life expectancy over the last several generations. People retiring today can typically expect to receive benefits for ten or twenty years longer than those who retired in the 1930s.

The demographic shift has put pressure on this system. The government is feeling the pinch, and so will recipients if benefits must be cut back. There is supposed to be a cost-of-living increase, but those don't seem to satisfy most retirees.

Federal policy has made the situation worse. As workers paid into the system, the government didn't invest the money so that it could build and grow a surplus. Instead, the government used those funds for other purposes, and now, it's trying to figure out how to put the money back.

Could Social Security be the biggest Ponzi scheme ever? Think about it. Bernie Madoff took money from the masses and paid it out to a few and was taking in billions until more and more people started losing money. Then, all of a sudden, he didn't have it to pay out, and he got caught and went to prison. Unfortunately, we can't hold anybody accountable for what's happening to our Social Security.

A Taste of Freedom

Few retirees these days imagine themselves sitting in a rocking chair on the porch. It doesn't work out that way. People entering retirement are hoping for freedom, however they might define that. They relish the thought of freedom to pursue interests and hobbies for which they lacked time while working; freedom to volunteer for worthy causes; freedom to spend time with the grandchildren. Some want freedom from the alarm clock, while many others want the freedom to pursue a new career or a new challenge. Many of our clients are starting new businesses.

Often, however, they find that freedom is taken away by economic necessity. They trusted the wrong advisor, took too much risk, and now it's difficult to make ends meet and they worry about emergencies, or what they saved has suffered such setbacks from market downturns that they now must go back to work at a job that pays much less than they once earned.

But whether from necessity or proclivity, today's retirees stay very busy with packed schedules. They travel, visit, play, volunteer. "Greg, I don't know how I ever had time to work," one client told me. Retirement can be a robust stage of life and far different from the leisurely pace you might imagine.

The Race Is Not to the Swift

Retirees, take note: you cannot run like a sprinter and expect to win the marathon. Let me emphasize again that in your retirement years, you should not be using the same strategies of money management that you used in your working years. Now is the time to pace yourself for a different kind of race.

In retirement, it's time to heed the new rules of the changed game. You are no longer making money for the future. You have arrived. When you worked, you contributed regularly to your investments and, as long as you felt your money was being managed well, you let your portfolio rise and fall with the market. If it rose, you celebrated. If it fell, you figured it was a chance to buy securities for a bargain. You felt confident that in the long run your investment chart would rise. Time was on your side. You could be more aggressive and take more chances.

When you're sixty or older, time isn't on your side anymore. Now, you have to "know that you know" that your income is going to be there. You can't afford to lose it. You not only need income-producing investments, but you also need money you can invest, untouched, at a higher rate to gain a return for the later years of your retirement. The

31

money that's invested in the market has time to catch up from losses without being depleted by withdrawals.

First and foremost, however, it is essential to set aside the money you need for your retirement income, because your income is your lifestyle.

Here, in the preservation phase of your life, think of yourself as a marathon runner. If you take off in a sprint, you may feel a youthful burst of energy, but you soon will be lagging. You need to conserve your resources so you have the stamina for the final victory.

"When the gates are all down and the signals are flashing and the whistle is screaming in vain and you stay on the tracks ignoring the facts well then you can't blame the wreck on the train."

"You Can't Blame the Train," lyrics by Terri Sharp, as sung by Don McLean

---

CHAPTER TWO

REPLACING THAT PAYCHECK

"Greg, how do I know?" It's a poignant question that I commonly hear when people come to see me about their retirement plans, and it's one that gets to a core fear: they just don't know whether their money will see them through. They're not confident that they are ready to retire—or if they already have taken that step, whether they might have to return to work.

When we have our talk about goals in the initial interview, that's when I hear the question: "Is my money going to last?" I cannot answer people until I hear what they hope to do with the rest of their lives. What are their expectations? And as I listen, I can quickly assess whether the goals are realistic.

Some of them have visited the major wire houses and brokers and seen fancy pie charts and heard predictions about what the market will do in the next however-many years.

"I've been told," a client might tell me, "that I could probably take out 4 or 5 percent of my money every year until I'm ninety-five, so I think I'm going to be okay."

"Is that good enough for you?" I respond. "Is just thinking you're going to be okay good enough? Or would you like to *know* for sure?"

Invariably, retirees want more than wishful thinking. So, we take a look at income goals and assets and run an analysis that determines the truth of the matter: whether their money will last as long as they do.

A Protected Income Stream

We test whether the financial house is in order, and the foundation of that house is protected income. That comes not only from Social Security and company pensions but also from a guaranteed lifelong income plan that we devise with the client—their own personal pension strategy. It could come from an IRA or 401(k), a brokerage account, or some other saving vehicle.

If Bob and Mary come to me and say, "We need $2,500 more per month to meet our lifestyle," I can explain how much money they need in their income plan to protect that cash flow. Our goal is to use the least amount of assets possible to protect the income that is needed.

When you take risk off the table and protect your income first, while providing for an appropriate amount of growth, you are on your way to a successful retirement. Protecting income is the most important aspect of a retirement plan. You must be crystal clear about the lifestyle you desire and realistic about whether your assets will support it. If there is a discrepancy and you do not resolve it, trouble lies ahead.

> When you take risk off the table and guarantee your income first, you are on your way to a successful retirement.

Goals Must Match Reality

I recently met with a couple who had saved about $600,000 between IRAs and 401(k)s in investments. They wanted to maintain the lifestyle they lived while they were both working, with a goal of $100,000 per year income in retirement. The husband had roughly $2,500 per month in Social Security, or $30,000 a year. The wife's was about half of that. They didn't have a pension. That meant that they had to draw $55,000 a year from their $600,000, or nearly 10 percent.

I told them, "You know, I can get you a 6 percent cash flow. I can generate roughly $36,000 a year for you, in addition to your other income, which would put you at $85,000 or $90,000 per year, but I can't get you to $100,000."

They seemed perplexed. "We should be able to earn 10 percent a year on our money," the husband declared. "Our broker says the market has averaged that over the last eighty years."

"It's just not realistic," I told them. "Maybe you should have that broker put that in writing for you." What they wanted, in other words, wasn't likely to happen—not without intolerable risk.

Safety versus Risk

Within the three worlds of money that I mentioned in the last chapter, there are different levels of risk.

Money invested in the banking world is safer; these asset classes include checking, savings, money market accounts, and CDs. Other safe investments include US treasuries and savings bonds, or fixed annuities, which are purchased through insurance companies. With these types of accounts, your principal is guaranteed. Bank accounts are guaranteed up to a stated amount by the Federal Deposit Insurance

Corporation (FDIC), and the federal government backs up treasuries and savings bonds.

Money invested in the brokerage world could be in mutual fund families, whose managers try to make your money grow within those funds; or it may be invested in the brokerage world, where stocks and bonds are traded; or you may have a variable annuity from an insurance company.

What people like about safe investments is that their principals are secured, but they dislike the risk of not keeping pace with inflation. They like the potential for a much better return in the growth world, but they are concerned, or should be, that they could lose their money.

In 1995, the hybrid world was created. Hybrid contracts, also called linked contracts, are designed to provide safety of principal, but they are also linked to a market index such as the S&P 500 to take advantage of growth opportunities.

The hybrid world began with the banks, which in the 1990s were losing so much money to the stock market that they created what they called the index-linked CD in order to compete. That money was not actually in the market, but the growth was linked to the index performance, and if the index went up, the investor would get part of the gain up to a cap of, say, 7 or 8 percent. If the index dropped, the investor would get zero gain—but wouldn't lose anything. CDs were not paying much at the time, so that was really attractive to CD buyers who wanted some extra gain but didn't want to take the risk.

Then, insurance companies came out with similar index-linked annuities. They employed the same idea: Your investment gained if the index rose, but if it dropped, you suffered no loss. Your principal was secure, but you had some potential to gain more than the traditional fixed annuity rate.

In 2007, this linked product was made even more attractive with the addition of guaranteed lifetime income benefits. Imagine a single annuity product with two sides growing simultaneously. One is based on the market index, rising if the index rises and remaining at zero if the index falls. That side works like the earlier index-based annuity. The other side is an income base and provides a guaranteed percentage of growth depending on the company that

> Hybrid contracts can give you a guaranteed income and growth without market risk. They can go a long way toward securing your retirment.

issues the annuity and the investor's age. Even if the fixed rates are down and the market is not going up, that side will rise every year. Then, when you decide to establish an income, the company will guarantee that income for as long as you and your spouse live.

Hybrid annuities give you growth potential without stock market risk as well as a protected income.* They can go a long way toward securing a retirement portfolio and providing an income that you know won't run out.

Wall Street has done an excellent job of trying to discredit annuities, but annuities are a legitimate financial tool if used for the right purpose and in the right instance. They allow you to commit fewer assets for providing income than if we follow the old Wall Street rule of 50 percent stocks/50 percent bonds and withdrawing 4 percent.

Recently, I met with a couple who had saved $3 million; to maintain their lifestyle, we needed to generate an additional $100,000 per year. The Wall Street 4 percent rule would have required $2.5 million to accomplish that goal. That only left $500,000 for their long-term growth. Instead, they chose a hybrid annuity with $1.6 million protected. That left $1.4 million in their growth bucket for long-term needs. This is a discussion that brokers who only sell stocks, bonds, and mutual funds don't want to have with you.

Wally's Lesson: You Can't Have It All

When I was growing up in the south end of Columbus, Ohio, I used to walk or ride my bike to a little store called Wally's Corner, at South High Street and Williams Road. Along the way, I'd collect empty pop bottles for their ten-cent deposits—money that people literally had thrown out the window. I cashed them in for candy and snacks.

I remember a sign above the door that said, "Low prices. Great service. Convenient. Pick any two." That holds true in the worlds of money. You have a choice among three benefits in your investments: growth potential, safety of principal, and 100 percent liquidity. But you can only pick two. You can't have it all. If you choose safety and liquidity, you lose growth potential. If you choose growth and liquidity, you lose safety. And if you choose growth and safety, you lose liquidity.

In the world of hybrid annuities, you are choosing the latter. You have growth potential, yet you have safety—a dollar-for-dollar backing of your money. But then, you find out that in return for that, the company will only let you withdraw 10 percent of your money per year without a fee. If you take out more, you will be penalized—and that's typically over an eight- to ten-year period.

In that way, hybrids clearly have strings attached. However, when you set up a lifetime guaranteed income plan, that restriction should not make a difference. As long as you understand where the strings are attached, all three worlds of money can be beneficial to a solid retirement plan. Think of the adage about not keeping all your eggs in one basket.

Beware: Sequence of Return Risk

If you wisely and methodically make use of all three worlds of money, you can craft a very secure retirement plan. Your immediate income should be drawn from the proper place. It's important that the accounts from which you withdraw it are protected. You want certainty that your income will be secure.

Therefore, you should not regularly tap into any money that you set aside for growth and that will be subjected to risk. You need to be able to let it ride the waves of the markets and grow over time. During the course of a decade, the market has proved that it can grow. But if you are taking money out of your account every month along the way, you can stymie that growth. You will be suffering the effects of reverse dollar cost averaging—the phenomenon that depleted the nest egg of the couple earlier in this chapter. The following charts illustrate this scenario:

Can Market Volatility Impact My Retirement?

Customer Name:	Mr. and Mrs. Client	
Investment Amount:	$1,000,000	
Index to Illustrate:	S&P 500	
Beginning Month/Year:	January - 2000	
Ending Month/Year:	January - 2024	
Annual Income Withdrawal:	4.00%	
Annual Income Withdrawal COLA:	0.00%	

Month	Year	Beginning Value	One-Year Index Return	Change in Value	Annual Withdrawal	Year End Value
January	2000	$1,000,000	-2.01%	($20,100)	$40,000	$939,900
January	2001	$939,900	-17.28%	($162,415)	$40,000	$737,485
January	2002	$737,485	-24.25%	($178,840)	$40,000	$518,645
January	2003	$518,645	32.13%	$166,641	$40,000	$645,286
January	2004	$645,286	4.42%	$28,522	$40,000	$633,808
January	2005	$633,808	8.38%	$53,113	$40,000	$646,921
January	2006	$646,921	12.34%	$79,830	$40,000	$686,751
January	2007	$686,751	-4.10%	($28,157)	$40,000	$618,594
January	2008	$618,594	-40.10%	($248,056)	$40,000	$330,538
January	2009	$330,538	30.02%	$99,228	$40,000	$389,766
January	2010	$389,766	19.74%	$76,940	$40,000	$426,706
January	2011	$426,706	0.47%	$2,006	$40,000	$388,712
January	2012	$388,712	15.94%	$61,961	$40,000	$410,673
January	2013	$410,673	18.96%	$77,864	$40,000	$448,537
January	2014	$448,537	11.95%	$53,600	$40,000	$462,137
January	2015	$462,137	-2.76%	($12,755)	$40,000	$409,382
January	2016	$409,382	17.42%	$71,314	$40,000	$440,696
January	2017	$440,696	23.92%	$105,414	$40,000	$506,110
January	2018	$506,110	-4.22%	($21,358)	$40,000	$444,752
January	2019	$444,752	19.27%	$85,704	$40,000	$490,456
January	2020	$490,456	15.16%	$74,353	$40,000	$524,809
January	2021	$524,809	21.57%	$113,201	$40,000	$598,010
January	2022	$598,010	-9.72%	($58,127)	$40,000	$499,883
January	2023	$499,883	0.00%	$0	$40,000	$459,883

Total Change in Account Value: -54.01%

Prepared By: Greg Taylor

The purpose of this illustration is to demonstrate the potential risks of depleting an account when annual withdrawals are combined with market volatility. This illustration shows hypothetical results of an account invested in a broad stock market index and does not account for the re-investment of dividends or any investment fees associated with an account. The index values used for the calculations are month-end closing values that are adjusted for dividends and splits and were obtained from Yahoo Finance. Calculations assume deferral of taxes. The Standard & Poors 500 (S&P 500) is an unmanaged group of securities considered to be representative of the stock market in general. The Dow Jones Industrial Average (DJIA) is a price-weighted average of 30 significant stocks traded on the New York Stock Exchange.

Can Market Volatility Impact My Retirement?

Customer Name:	Mr. and Mrs. Client	
Investment Amount:	$1,000,000	
Index to Illustrate:	S&P 500	
Beginning Month/Year:	January - 2000	
Ending Month/Year:	January - 2024	
Annual Income Withdrawal:	$0	
Annual Income Withdrawal COLA:	0.00%	

Month	Year	Beginning Value	One-Year Index Return	Change in Value	Annual Withdrawal	Year End Value
January	2000	$1,000,000	-2.01%	($20,100)	$0	$979,900
January	2001	$979,900	-17.28%	($169,327)	$0	$810,573
January	2002	$810,573	-24.25%	($196,564)	$0	$614,009
January	2003	$614,009	32.13%	$197,281	$0	$811,290
January	2004	$811,290	4.42%	$35,859	$0	$847,149
January	2005	$847,149	8.38%	$70,991	$0	$918,140
January	2006	$918,140	12.34%	$113,298	$0	$1,031,438
January	2007	$1,031,438	-4.10%	($42,289)	$0	$989,149
January	2008	$989,149	-40.10%	($396,649)	$0	$592,500
January	2009	$592,500	30.02%	$177,869	$0	$770,369
January	2010	$770,369	19.74%	$152,071	$0	$922,440
January	2011	$922,440	0.47%	$4,335	$0	$926,775
January	2012	$926,775	15.94%	$147,728	$0	$1,074,503
January	2013	$1,074,503	18.96%	$203,726	$0	$1,278,229
January	2014	$1,278,229	11.95%	$152,748	$0	$1,430,977
January	2015	$1,430,977	-2.76%	($39,495)	$0	$1,391,482
January	2016	$1,391,482	17.42%	$242,396	$0	$1,633,878
January	2017	$1,633,878	23.92%	$390,824	$0	$2,024,702
January	2018	$2,024,702	-4.22%	($85,442)	$0	$1,939,260
January	2019	$1,939,260	19.27%	$373,695	$0	$2,312,955
January	2020	$2,312,955	15.16%	$350,644	$0	$2,663,599
January	2021	$2,663,599	21.57%	$574,538	$0	$3,238,137
January	2022	$3,238,137	-9.72%	($314,747)	$0	$2,923,390
January	2023	$2,923,390	0.00%	$0	$0	$2,923,390

Total Change in Account Value: 192.34%

Prepared By: Greg Taylor

The purpose of this illustration is to demonstrate the potential risks of depleting an account when annual withdrawals are combined with market volatility. This illustration shows hypothetical results of an account invested in a broad stock market index and does not account for the re-investment of dividends or any investment fees associated with an account. The index values used for the calculations are month-end closing values that are adjusted for dividends and splits and were obtained from Yahoo Finance. Calculations assume deferral of taxes. The Standard & Poors 500 (S&P 500) is an unmanaged group of securities considered to be representative of the stock market in general. The Dow Jones Industrial Average (DJIA) is a price-weighted average of 30 significant stocks traded on the New York Stock Exchange.

For example, let's say you have a $1 million portfolio and are paying 1 percent in fees and are withdrawing 5 percent a year. Let's say the market suffers a 15 percent drop for the year. That's a total depletion of 21 percent of the portfolio's value. If that happens only two years in a row, that's 42 percent. You now need a 74 percent gain to make that up. But wait: If you still need to be taking out that 5 percent of the original million, you need more than a 74 percent gain. Actually, to withdraw the equivalent amount of money, you need to take out 8 percent, since you now have only $580,000 left. So, that's 74 percent, plus 8 percent, plus 1 percent in fees—for a total of a 83 percent gain, you will need, just because the market dropped 15 percent, two years in a row.

> You must not regularly tap into money that you set aside for growth and is subject to risk.

You may never recover from that the rest of your life. Did your broker ever explain that to you? Or did the broker lead you to believe that the strategy of your working years still made sense for retirement? When you earn a paycheck and set investment money aside every week or two, you are experiencing dollar cost averaging—which, unlike its reverse, can dramatically build your portfolio over time. You begin your career in your twenties, you marry, you buy a house, you have children—and all the while, those contributions grow, with retirement on the distant horizon. When the market rises, your portfolio blooms. When it falters, that just means a dollar buys more of an investment that will rise later. In other words, in a down market, your dollar buys a bargain. In an up market, your dollar buys less, but your earlier bargains flourish. Over the years, your investments average out to a healthy gain. That's the beauty of dollar cost averaging.

Dollar cost averaging is a great strategy for while you're working, and those who recommended it for that phase of your life were certainly your advocates. And if, along the way, your health didn't fail or your employer didn't move overseas, you one day find yourself approaching retirement with a sizable nest egg. Perhaps you have even saved—eureka!—a million dollars. Certainly, you may tell yourself, you safely can take out 5 percent every year—and the market that has been so good to you will surely make that up, and more. You feel more than set for life. But as we have seen in such excruciating detail, if you keep all that money in the market, it's more like a setup for financial disaster. All those decades of hard work to amass your million or more, and you can lose a big part of it in just a few consecutive bear years. It happened to many, and not so very long ago.

What the Brokers Tell Us

Brokers use the market to make money. They do a great job of helping us position our assets from a young age to grow our money over time. But they see the stock market as the sole answer when it comes to financial strategies, and they're convinced that the same strategies that you used when you were younger will continue to work when you transition to retirement. They haven't come to grips with the fact that the stock market isn't the only answer for every retirement portfolio because of two things that can happen: market stagnation and market declines. Either of those can be a real problem for your portfolio when you're in retirement.

Now, it is true that earlier in life, when you're in the accumulation phase and you're working and you're putting money aside for your future, you do need to have money in growth and can afford those risks. You're investing money regularly and not touching it. But as we have seen, once you get to retirement, your focus needs to shift.

Brokers also tell us that if we diversify our assets, we will be just fine. In your 401(k), for example, keep a reasonable mix of stocks and bonds, depending on your risk tolerance and age, they say. They present that as a way to balance your risk and diversify your investments.

"Greg, all that happened for me," a potential client told me at the time when I explained that diversification wasn't working. "It just spread the pain around in a whole lot of different places."

This is the lesson: Diversification isn't a matter of spreading your money around in different stock market investments. To truly diversify, your investments should be allocated within the three worlds of money that we discussed earlier in the book: banking, brokerage, and insurance.

You need impartial advice, not the standard "wisdom" that you hear from the finance houses or stockbrokers. What you hear about keeping your money at risk is not necessarily wise for your nest egg. If you follow the wrong advice, you will find yourself siphoning away your retirement funds to the point where you may have to return to work just to get by.

That is what happens when your money is at risk in a flagging economy. It doesn't have to be that way. There are ways to handle your nest egg so that it will not crack open. Again, here is a fundamental truth that I cannot emphasize enough: the financial strategies of your working years may not be suitable for your retirement years, when what you have is what must see you through. You no longer have time to just hold tight and hope for the best. It's time to have more purpose in your planning.

Staggering Statistics

If you need evidence of why you must act now, consider these statistics: As of 2019, 40.6 percent of all US households where the head of household is between thirty-five and sixty-four are projected to run short of money in retirement, according to a study by the Employee Benefit Research Institute. Looking at individuals, the average retirement savings shortfall for those aged sixty to sixty-four ranges from $12,640 per individual for widowers to $15,782 for widows. It increases to $24,905 for single males and $62,127 for single females.[1]

The fact that millions and millions of people who are retired can face this problem is a big issue—and it need not work out that way. The statistics underscore the importance of having a plan in place so that you know you won't run out.

From 1982 through 2000, we saw the greatest bull market in our country's history. Most of the people who are retiring today began putting money aside in their IRAs or 401(k)s or other investments during that time. To them, what happened during the 1980s and 1990s still seems to be the norm. That's what they experienced for most of their investment life.

> The financial strategies of your working years are not suitable for your retirement years, when what you have is what must see you through.

Most of today's advisors began their careers during that period, so that bull market became their normal too. That is partly why so many

---

1   Jack VanDerhei, "Retirement Savings Shortfalls: Evidence from EBRI's 2019 Retirement Security Projection Model," March 7, 2019, https://www.ebri.org/content/retirement-savings-shortfalls-evidence-from-ebri-s-2019-retirement-security-projection-model.

stockbrokers have such bad advice today for retirees. Often, they lack the historical perspective that engenders financial wisdom. As a result, you so often hear their dubious counsel: "Just hang in there. The market always comes back. Don't worry about it. It's going to come back. Buy and hold. Don't worry about strategy. Just buy and hold. The market's going to go up."

History's Way of Repeating Itself

During the 1980s and 1990s, that wasn't a bad strategy at all. But a look at how the markets have performed over many generations will quickly demonstrate that the romping economy that we saw at the end of the last century was not typical. Retiring boomers must brace themselves for less than booming times.

For example, from 1900 to around 1923, we were in a sideways market. It barely grew at all during that period. Then, from 1923 to 1928, we experienced a great bull market. Of course, in 1929, it crashed, heralding the Great Depression. It recovered about halfway five years later and then stayed pretty level until 1949. It took another twenty years to regain the rest. Think about what your retirement would have been like in those various times.

From 1949 until 1964, the market was in a bull pattern again, so if you were retired during those years, you may have done well. But from 1964 until 1982, the market averaged 0.007 percent a year. What if you were retired then? There were ups and downs, but unless you bought at the exact right time and

> The romping economy of the 1990s was far from normal. Retiring boomers must brace themselves for less than booming times.

46

sold at the exact right time, your portfolio was a mess after those seventeen years.

Then, we had the greatest run-up of our history, 1982–2000. Since 2000, how have we fared? On January 14 of that year, the Dow was at 11,723 points. It dropped way down in 2002 and then came back up in 2007 where it was over 14,000 points. It dropped down to just over 6,000 in 2009 and then began recovering. But look at how long it has taken us. If you're retired, can you wait several years?

When you take your blinders off and look at the historical performance of the market, it's clear that the rise of the late 1990s wasn't normal. In truth, there have been more down and sideways periods than up periods. Research by Rydex SGI shows that what is closer to normal are long, flat periods, with some long declining periods, with an occasional bull market.

From 1896 to 1906, we saw a bull market with a 148.92 percent cumulative return. From 1906 to 1924, we saw eighteen years where the cumulative return was minus 4.29 percent. The Dow index showed an annualized loss of 0.24 percent per year, so if you held your stocks during that period, you would have lost more than 4 percent of your money. From 1929 through 1954—a quarter century—you would have gained only 0.07 percent per year on average, or less than 1.7 percent in that period. When you account for inflation, that means you would have lost a great deal of your money by buying and holding.

The stock market, like history, has a way of repeating itself. If you look at a chart of the market performance since its inception, you could focus on any series of years. Depending on where you put the beginning and the end of that focus, investing in the market would either be a great idea or a frightening one.

It's often said that the market returns, on average, 10 percent a year for the long term. According to a recent DALBAR study, the average equity fund investor only saw annual returns of only 6.81 percent on average over the last thirty years. If you were in stocks and bonds, the return would have been even lower. Now, more than ever, it's important to see if the returns you're getting are actually worth the risks you're taking. Do you know what you're getting for the risks you're taking?

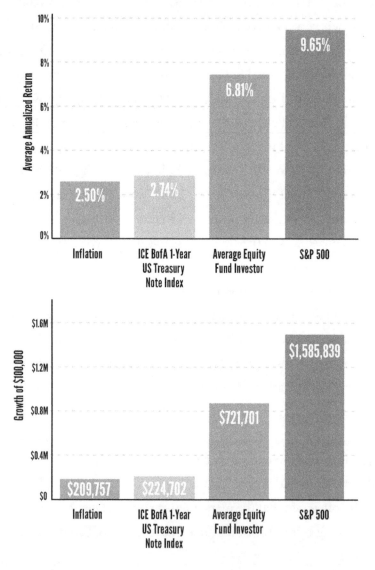

The Dalbar Study: Average Equity Fund Investor vs. Indexes Over 30 Years
30 Years (1/1/1993 - 12/31/2022)

Whenever somebody suggests you look at the long term, consider how long is acceptable for you. Depending on where we are in the economic cycle when you retire, the "long term" could be too long for you to endure.

The New Normal

We have seen the new normal. It began with the dawn of the millennium, and some economists and investment managers, including PIMCO's Bill Gross, expected low stock and bond returns to linger for years.

Investors need a wake-up call. If you profited from the economy of 1982–2000, be thankful but don't expect a repeat performance. If you have retired in this century, you also have entered a new normal for the economy—and it's a far cry from the 1990s, when it seemed monkeys could throw darts to choose stocks and they'd get fabulous returns.

The Dow Jones, between January 2000 and the spring of 2012, grew only about 10 percent. That's 0.84 percent per year. What do you suppose would happen if you had all your assets in the market and you were depending on being able to withdraw 5 percent per year from your portfolio? If you were averaging such a minuscule amount in that period, and were paying fees and taxes on your earnings to boot, and at the same time needed that account as your source of income, you are probably in dire condition.

When Indicators Point the Wrong Way

Money managers and economists use an assortment of hypotheses and theories and pie charts on which they base projections for how the market should behave, based on indicators. And those can point the wrong way.

One day in 2007, a couple was sitting with me in my office and the man was telling me he was still heavily invested in technologies. His wife had a look of fright in her eyes as he spoke.

"Greg," he said, "there's just no logical reason for why technologies shouldn't be exploding."

"But they're not," I offered. "And the bottom line is, you've lost 60 percent of your life savings, and your wife is scared to death. She's about to have a nervous breakdown. Whether or not logic says it should or shouldn't be happening, you're about to lose it all, my friend, because you weren't looking at what's all around you."

It isn't about logic, and it's not about predictions. At the end of 2007, *Business Week* listed thirteen money managers who were predicting an average rise in the S&P 500 index for the next year of 9.8 percent. It fell 38.5 percent.

"For forty years, I followed a system that simply does not work," Alan Greenspan, the former Federal Reserve Chairman, said in 2009.

"The financial crisis was avoidable and was caused by market participants and regulators following flawed market theories," billionaire George Soros said in October 2010, as quoted by the Financial Crisis Inquiry Commission on its website.

Such theories base future outlook on past experiences—but look at the situation at the end of 2002, when the NASDAQ had dropped severely over the previous two years. Investors who had thought they could get NASDAQ stock at bargain basement prices soon learned it would tumble far further. Or look at 2020, when COVID-19 spread around the world and the S&P 500 dropped 23 percent; just when it seemed it was recovering, it dropped 23 percent again as a result of a global decline in risk assets. During these years, many retirees put their plans on hold and are still working to recover.

Trying to predict the future and predict the markets is crazy, no matter how many initials you have after your name or what your address is on Wall Street. Of one thing you can be certain: there's going to be uncertainty.

The Truth about Bonds

The key to surviving during uncertainty is to diversify your investments—and as we have discussed, that does not mean spreading your risk around in the stock and bond markets. It means carefully weighing your situation and deciding how much, if any, should be risked at all—and how much should be kept absolutely safe.

The older you get, according to the stockbrokers, the more you should diversify by shifting to bonds. The idea is that at age thirty, you might have nothing in bonds, but by age fifty, you'll want perhaps a third of your portfolio invested in them, with the rest in equities.

Bond values have an inverse relationship to interest rates. Let's say I bought a bond today at 3 percent (my par rate) and paid $1,000. With the interest rate remaining at 3 percent, I should be able to sell it for $1,000. But if the rate dropped to 2 percent, my bond's value should command a premium price, so I should be able to sell it for $1,200.

On the other hand, if the interest rate were to rise to 4 percent, who would want to buy my bond for even the amount I paid for it? Why would they pay $1,000 for my 3 percent bond when they could get a 4 percent bond for the same price? If I needed to sell my bond, I'd have to offer a discount, perhaps letting it go for $800.

The problem is that there has been such a lack of consumer confidence in recent years that even bonds that should be selling at a premium have been selling at a discount—not because the rate increased, but because consumers lacked confidence in the bond holder. Many companies and municipalities have faltered on their bonds. The risk of default is quite real. With the recent environment of low interest rates, those entering the world of bonds run a significant risk that those rates will rise and their bond will be nearly worthless. Rates have been unlikely to fall further, so there hasn't been a lot of room for bonds to go down in price.

If you are looking to buy bonds as a shelter against risk, you may want to think again. According to a 2022 article from the *Wall Street Journal*, "The Bloomberg U.S. Aggregate bond index dropped 13%, easily outdoing its previous worst year in data going back to the 1970s, when it declined 2.9% in 1994."[2]

Rule of 100

Investment advisors often cite the "Rule of 100" as a way to decide how much of your portfolio to allocate between stocks and bonds, in the world of risk. It goes like this: Subtract your age from one hundred. The result is the maximum percentage you should have in the stock market. If you are sixty, for example, no more than 40 percent of your money should be invested in stocks. The rest, the theory goes, should be in bonds.

But we believe you need to take a much different approach. We believe you need to start with what you need to achieve and then find the right mix of strategies that are best suited to achieving those things. We want to fit your retirement portfolio to what you need rather than trying to fit you into a 60/40 mold.

---

2   Sam Goldfarb, "For Battered Bonds, Threats of Further Losses Linger," *The Wall Street Journal*, January 2, 2023, https://www.wsj.com/articles/ for-battered-bonds-threats-of-further-losses-linger-11672602373.

A retirement portfolio needs to be far more than just how much is in stocks and how much is in bonds. We work with ninety-year-olds that need absolutely no income, like risk, and have the majority of their portfolios in equities, but we also work with sixty-year-olds who can no longer afford to take that risk with the amount of income that is required for their retirement.

Therefore, one of our guiding principles is that investment decisions should not be made outside the context of your plan. Instead, we ask: What do you need your money to do in retirement? The answer to that then guides us as to how much should be in what type of investment, whether it's in banking, brokerage, or the insurance world.

Variable Annuities

It's particularly important to be aware of a highly popular financial product that can threaten your portfolio. I have seen the results among clients who come to me for help at Legacy Retirement Group. Most of them do not understand what they were sold. Some think they have an index-linked annuity, when in fact they have a variable annuity. A false belief about a financial product is worse than ignorance.

Variable annuities are an insurance product that has subaccounts. They're called subaccounts, but they look like mutual funds within a variable annuity. It's not uncommon for variable annuity fees to total between 3 and 5 percent annually, when you add in the riders. The financial world offers much safer and less expensive options, ones that variable annuities do not begin to rival.

Although a standard annuity is clearly in the world of safety, a variable annuity is well within the world of market risk. If the market loses, so do you. And the proprietary funds that are typically pushed within the variable annuities will generally underperform a traditional index. When you consider the high fees, you have so much working against you that it's almost impossible to make up for a down market. You get to the place where you feel imprisoned by the account, as if you can never get your principal out of it unless you die and your heirs get the death benefit.

Remember that the average mutual fund costs between 1 and 2 percent annually in fees. The average investment advisor fee is about 1 percent. So, if you are paying 1 percent inside your mutual fund and 1 percent to your advisor, that means that over a twenty-year period of retirement, 40 percent of your retirement dollars go to the broker on Wall Street. The investment prospectus doesn't make that clear—the information is there, but it seems hidden, and it would take a Philadelphia lawyer to understand it.

Variable annuities remain highly popular for a not-so-good reason: insurance agents and brokers receive very high commissions. I could offer variable annuities to my clients if I had the inclination, but I feel that would be a grave disservice. They can do so much better with the new generation of hybrid income annuities and other more secure options.

How can you make sure you are on the way to sound financial footing? Here, in brief, are some fundamental and crucial steps to take:

1. Have your portfolio tested to make sure that it is structured properly for retirement.

2. Have a written plan that focuses on being efficient with your investments, income, and taxes, and making sure that you are protecting yourself from things like future inflation, healthcare costs, and those kinds of concerns.

3. Make sure your investments can hedge for inflation and avoid excessive fees. Together with market losses, inflation and fees can add up to a devastating percentage.

4. Find a good registered investment advisor. A registered investment advisor has a fiduciary responsibility to only do what's in your best interest. He is working for you.

Guarantees apply to certain insurance and annuity products (not securities, variable, or investment advisory products), including optional benefits, and are subject to product terms, exclusions and limitations, and the insurer's claims—paying ability and financial strength of the issuing insurance company.

"No taxes can be devised which are not more or less inconvenient and unpleasant."
—George Washington

CHAPTER THREE

AVOIDING TAX TRAPS

It has been said that the difference between tax evasion and tax avoidance is about twenty years. Within that thick rule book, you can find many ways to avoid taxes on your income and estate. If you follow the tax code, you are not breaking the law, either legally or ethically.

But the government is not going to tell you everything that you can do. At tax time, you aren't going to get a pamphlet from the Internal Revenue Service explaining how to cut back on what you owe. As long as you work within the guidelines, however, you can legally pay much less, depending on whether you take advantage of some of the provisions. If you do, you get a break. If you don't, you get to pay more.

In other words, there is a financial risk to being uninformed and unprepared. You could fall into a tax trap if you manage your money inefficiently and end up paying the government a small fortune, unnecessarily. You won't get a thank-you note from the IRS for sending that extra money.

For example, when the exemption from federal estate tax is high, it is possible to lock in that advantage through strategic gifting strategies. You hold on to that exemption forever, even after the government lowers the amount you can exclude from taxes. You can still maintain a certain amount of control over those gifts. But the government isn't going to show you how to do that. The mistake of failing to plan could cost your heirs hundreds of thousands or even millions of dollars.

> The government isn't going to show you how to save on taxes. Failing to plan could cost your heirs millions.

Besides estate taxes, your annual income taxes can take a mighty toll on your nest egg if you fail to plan efficiently. If you don't shelter your money from Uncle Sam's grasp, you can lose much of what you need to live well during your retirement.

The Four-Letter Word

Back in 2011, during an interview on a national radio show, former comptroller general of the US General Accountability Office, David Walker, said that future tax rates would have to double or our country would go bankrupt. There was a four-letter word that convinced him of this, and he invited listeners to call with their guesses. Ultimately, nobody guessed the word. Do you know what it was? Math. According to the math, Walker said, taxes will have to double in order to pay the national debt, which at the time was $14 trillion. Since then, he has continued to spread his message to anyone who will listen, and the national debt has continued to grow exponentially.

Part of the problem is underfunded government liabilities like Medicare and Medicaid but especially Social Security. In 1935, when

Social Security was enacted by Franklin D. Roosevelt as part of the New Deal with America, there were approximately forty-two workers for every person collecting Social Security, and they couldn't collect it until age sixty-five. At the time, the average life expectancy of Americans was only age sixty-two. The government didn't really anticipate that the average American would live long enough to even draw Social Security, and those that did only collected for a few years before they passed away.

Today, there are only around three workers for everyone collecting Social Security, and life expectancy is now in the late seventies, so there are people who collect Social Security for twenty or thirty years. Add to that the population explosion of the baby boom generation in the wake of World War II, and those children

> Nationally known and well-spoken CPA Ed Slott refers to the upcoming tax situation in our country as a tax time bomb. Others refer to our tax situation in our country as a runaway freight train.

born as part of the boom have had fewer children than their parents. All of that has contributed to the math.

In short, Social Security was never intended to be a retirement program, and it certainly wasn't intended to be our main source of income when we retire. The math behind the Social Security problem is just one example of the broader crisis that's facing our country today.

Legislative Risk

Over the years, our elected officials have made more and more promises to the American people on things that they really don't have the money to pay for, resulting in those underfunded obligations. The government spends roughly eighty cents out of every dollar it collects on four items: Social Security, Medicare, Medicaid, and interest on the national debt.

Looking back at taxes, in the 1940s, the highest tax rate was 94 percent if you made more than $200,000 per year.[3] Granted, the average American didn't make that much, but that rate was unprecedented considering that only a decade earlier, the tax rate on the same income was only 58 percent. Could history have a way of repeating itself? Certainly, it could. When times were tough in America, as they were after World War II, the government raised taxes.

Today, the highest tax bracket in America is 37 percent. A couple making up to $383,900 per year would be in the 24 percent tax bracket. So, right now, we're in some of the lowest tax rates that we've seen in our country.

But while the national debt was $14 trillion in 2011, as a country, today we have almost $34 trillion in debt. With a debt like that, tax rates could definitely go up. Not only do we have to worry about future tax rates, but we also have to worry about the government changing the rules. It's called legislative risk.

Recent legislation looked to requiring the wealthy to start taking required minimum distributions (RMDs) right away, and it was proposed that 50 percent would need to be taken out every year. RMDs are the minimum amounts the government requires you to withdraw from your retirement accounts each year starting at age seventy-three, whether you need the money or not. The legislation didn't pass, but that shows you that America's retirement savings are

---

3   Tax Foundation, "Historical U.S. federal individual income tax rates & brackets, 1862-2021," August 24, 2021, https://taxfoundation.org/data/all/federal/historical-income-tax-rates-brackets/.

on the radar. The people who have worked the hardest, sacrificed the most, and been successful are the ones that are on the radar. Legislators talk about taxing the wealthy, but while there are only a few billionaires in America, there are several million millionaires.

If the government can tax us on things like our healthcare, what else might it tax us on? The country is almost $32 trillion in debt, and there is a little over $32 trillion in tax-deferred accounts.

What it all adds up to is this: now, more than ever, we need to be mindful of paying taxes today and protecting our future. Because more than healthcare, market volatility, inflation, or anything else, the biggest risks to our income in retirement are going to be taxes and legislative changes—and they're both unavoidable.

Replacement for Pensions

Not all that long ago, many retirees felt confidence in the pensions they would receive from decades of dedicated work with their company. Such pensions are rare today. What happened?

To a large extent, it comes down to competitive prices and the push by corporate America to lower costs. Many companies shifted work to other countries, and with the threat of further job losses, the "today" mentality replaced the "tomorrow" mentality in labor negotiations. Pension contributions suffered, and the plans began to disappear.

Individual retirement plans that allowed income-tax deductions for contributions were introduced in the 1970s and originally were restricted to those not covered by an employment-based retirement plan. That restriction was dropped in the 1980s except for higher-earning workers. Deferred-tax retirement plans began to replace pensions. They were sold to the public as a huge boon for their retirement planning.

The growth of IRAs and 401(k)s offered investors a tax-deferred way of saving for retirement, with the belief that they would be in a lower tax bracket then. No longer did they need to pay taxes each year on investment earnings.

It Pays to Be Wary

Imagine yourself in a year like 2008, needing to borrow $10,000. The banks aren't lending money, and your relatives and friends won't answer your calls. Then, you meet someone who smiles broadly, clutches your hand, and says, "I like you. Sure, I'll lend you $10,000. I'll cut you a check right now—cash it and enjoy it."

Before you say "yes," I would hope you would press for a few details—namely, what interest rate will this lender charge, and what will be the terms of this loan?

Suppose you hear this in response: "There, there, don't worry about it for now. We'll get together later and talk about that stuff. I'll let you know when I need the money back, and we'll figure out all the back interest payments."

Fools fall in. You're wiser than that.

But consider this: Many of you who are reading this right now have already taken that loan. It's called an IRA. Or a 401(k). It's called a 403(b), or a deferred compensation plan. Uncle Sam in effect has lent us money for our accounts but controls when and how much we have to take out, and he has a right to change what percentage he's going to charge us when we do.

If you have a million dollars in your IRA today, and you were putting that in over a twenty-year period, it would be fair to say that money doubled, maybe twice or at least one and a half times. You probably only put, say, $300,000 of your money in the million-dollar IRA. If the average working tax rate is 25 percent, that means Uncle Sam loaned you $75,000 in the form of a tax deferral. He'll want that money back at some point.

We have been misled to think that we will pay a much lower tax, or be in a lower tax bracket, when we retire. In 2022, the government announced that IRA holders would not be required to take a withdrawal that year. It would be a one-time exemption, and people thought they were being dealt a favor. Compassion? Hardly. The value of those accounts was down by half, and the government didn't want to take a discount on the taxes.

New Tax Strategies

When we look at your retirement plan, we want to look at a tax diversity strategy for your retirement income, an income plan in which some of your money will be taxed at lower rates. We want to look at ways to shift some of your resources into investment vehicles that will produce tax-free income.

A new way of looking at taxes starts by reexamining some of your presumptions. You may have believed, for example, that your IRA or 401(k) was a home-run hit, in which you could keep on deferring taxes until the day you started taking money out of the account—that day when, as you were assured, you would be in a much lower tax bracket. It's just not true now. People are taking that money out, and it's putting them into higher tax brackets. And Uncle Sam gets an additional bonus from you: the money you withdraw from those accounts is counted toward the amount you are allowed to earn before half your Social Security benefit is taxed.

Three decades ago, tax rates were high and people did feel a great incentive to defer the burden by investing in IRAs and 401(k)s and other means. More recently, the tax leverage benefits of deferring haven't been as compelling. As an example, between 1979 and 1980, anything over $11,900 was in the 21 percent tax bracket. When you earned over $20,200, you were in the 28 percent tax bracket. If you earned over $60,000, you were in the 54 percent tax bracket. If you earned $215,400, you were in the 70 percent tax bracket.

Today, up to $383,900 is in the 24 percent bracket. The highest tax bracket is 37 percent.

We are in a historically low income-tax era—and as deficits and financial crises pile up, that era is likely to end. The top tax in the past century averaged over 60 percent. We have become accustomed to paying far less, but we are seeing the push upward. In such a climate, deferral means waiting for higher taxes.

Taxable, Tax-Deferred, Tax-Free Funnels

It is important to understand the distinction between investments that are taxable, tax-free, and tax-deferred, and how each can fit into your retirement portfolio, both now and for the long haul because the effect on the growth of your portfolio can be profound. I talk about these in terms of funnels.

With the taxable funnel, you pay taxes before the money goes in, as it goes through the funnel, and on any gains. A taxable asset is one in which the gain or dividend earned is subject to tax each year. Assets in the taxable funnel may be interest-bearing savings accounts, CDs, or brokerage accounts. Savings and CDs are taxed on earnings every year; at year's end, you get a Form 1099 that tells you how much income you have to claim to Uncle Sam. On brokerage accounts, you pay taxes on dividends for those stocks that you hold, or capital gains on those that you sell. Congress has even proposed that we pay tax on unrealized capital gains, which means that we wouldn't even have to sell our securities in order to owe the tax. As I write this book, that proposal has not passed, but anytime the government proposes something like that, it means it's on their radar and it's something that will definitely be on the table again. In other words, the money we've worked hard for and saved is definitely something that legislators are looking at as a way to pay for their spending. With the taxable funnel, there is never an escape from taxation.

Then, there is the tax-deferred funnel, which is where most Americans have most of their money. This funnel contains tax-deferred annuities, IRAs, 401(k)s, 403(b)s, or 457 deferred compensation plans. For most of our working years, we've been taught not to pay tax today, but to delay it and pay our taxes later, when it's assumed our rate will be lower. Our CPAs, who are typically tax preparers, not planners, want to be our heroes so they tell us we can lower our taxes now by fully funding our tax-deferred accounts. Seems like sound advice, right? We've all bought into this over the years, including me.

But why are we delaying taxes to the unknown when we have some of the lowest tax rates in history? To me, that's like the loan I talked about earlier where you "discuss the terms later." In my mind, tax-deferred accounts are just loans from Uncle Sam. With a government that can't or won't stop spending; our country going from $14 to over $34 trillion in debt in just twelve short years; and Medicare, Medicaid, and Social Security being so underfunded, there's a real chance we could end up paying way more taxes later than what we saved by delaying our tax.

That brings us to the tax-free funnel. In the tax-free funnel, you pay all of the taxes before you go through the funnel, your interest and growth are tax-free, and as long as you follow all the applicable rules, everything you withdraw is tax-free. The tax-free funnel allows you to pay your tax bill upfront and then everything else is tax-free.

Tax Pitfalls

Something else to consider with each of the different funnels is the impact on Social Security benefits. For instance, one unintended problem with the tax-deferred funnel is that it can cause you to pay taxes on Social Security.

Currently, single filers must pay taxes on up to 50 percent of their Social Security benefits for a combined income of $25,000 to $34,000; over that amount, you may pay income taxes on up to 85 percent of benefits. For married couples filing jointly, the tax on 50 percent of Social Security income applies to a combined income of $32,000 to $44,000, and the taxes on 85 percent is on a combined income of more than $44,000.[4] That income includes anything that you pull out of your tax-deferred account. In other words, you may pay taxes on the tax-deferred money that you're taking out as income, and if you exceed certain income thresholds, you will also pay taxes on your Social Security benefits.

We pay income taxes at certain margins: part of your income is taxed at 10 percent, part at 12 percent, then at 22 percent if your earnings exceed the 12 percent, and so on. With normal income, currently, a married couple filing jointly in the 12 percent tax bracket can make up to $94,300. If that couple makes $94,310, the extra $10

---

4   Amelia Josephson, "Is Social Security Taxable?" SmartAsset, last modified July 25, 2023, accessed September 16, 2023, https://smartasset.com/retirement/is-social-security-income-taxable.

would be taxed at the margin of 22 percent. However, with Social Security, if the couple's income is $94,301, then the entire amount is taxed at the higher rate.

2024 Tax Brackets

TAX RATE	SINGLE FILERS	MARRIED COUPLES FILING JOINTLY	MARRIED COUPLES FILING SEPERATELY	HEAD OF HOUSEHOLD
10%	$11,600 or less	$23,000 or less	$11,600 or less	$16,550 or less
12%	$11,601 to $47,150	$23,201 to $94,300	$11,601 to $47,150	$16,551 to $63,100
22%	$47,151 to $100,525	$94,301 to $201,050	$47,141 to $100,525	$63,101 to $100,500
24%	$100,526 to $191,950	$201,051 to $383,900	$100,526 to $191,150	$100,501 to $191,150
32%	$191,951 to $243,725	$383,901 to $487,450	$191,151 to $243,725	$191,151 to $243,700
35%	$243,726 to $609,350	$487,451 to $731,200	$243,276 to $365, 600	$243,701 to $609,350
37%	$609,351 or more	$731,201 or more	$365,601 or more	$609,351 or more

Source: Internal Revenue Service

With assets like the Roth IRA, Roth 401(k)s, and Roth 403(b), taxes are paid before the money is put in, it grows tax-free, and as long as you follow all the rules, it comes out tax-free. When you later pull that money out for income in retirement, it will not impact taxes on your Social Security.

For instance, if you're a married couple with $60,000 per year, half of which is $30,000 in Social Security, that is less than the $32,000 where taxes on Social Security begin. If all of your other income comes out of a tax-free Roth account, then you will not owe taxes on your Social Security. At that point, you would have a tax-free retirement. Now, if you have a pension that adds $10,000 per year to the equation, that brings the taxable amount up from $30,000 to $40,000, which is over the $32,000 that Social Security allows. That would mean paying tax on 50 percent of Social Security benefits; but since the rest of the income is from a tax-free Roth, then at least you don't have to pay tax on 85 percent of your Social Security.

If the same couple were to pull $30,000 per year more out of a traditional IRA—considerably over the limit—then they would be looking at paying tax on 85 percent of their Social Security. In fact, with $30,000 Social Security plus $10,000 in pension and another $30,000 from a tax-deferred IRA, you're now in the 22 percent bracket and not only will you pay tax on 85 percent of your Social Security, but all of it will also be taxed at 22 percent.

But consider this: through carefully designed life insurance investments, retirees can devise a highly favorable retirement plan that will allow them to convert tax-deferred assets into a death benefit. Not only are they able to pass on a sizable sum tax-free to their heirs, but they can make tax-free withdrawals for annual income or to make major purchases.

Unlike a Roth or municipal bond, when you take income from life insurance, it's considered a tax-free loan. It's not a loan from your cash value; it's a loan against your cash value, which means that even the money that you took out the previous year as a loan still has the potential to earn interest this year because you didn't actually pull it from the cash value. Even though you are charged interest on that loan, there is the potential for it to earn more interest than you're being charged—you could actually earn interest on money that you've already spent.

To some clients, that scenario sounds too good to be true, but it is one of those little-known facts about the tax code. Those who set up the right kind of program can create a tax-free benefit for their loved ones and also provide tax-free withdrawals for themselves. And the money they withdraw does not count against how much they are allowed to earn before their Social Security benefit is taxed.

That doesn't mean that all of your money should be in the tax-free funnel. You will actually need some of your assets to be in a taxable funnel, and there are also reasons to keep some in a tax-deferred funnel. For instance, if your Social Security plus your required minimum distribution (RMD) is under the limit for Social Security taxation, then it might make sense to still keep some money in a tax-deferred account.

At Legacy Retirement Group, we calculate to see how much should be in each of the funnels—the taxable, the tax-deferred, and the tax-free—and through what we call an RMD Report, we can look at how taxes will impact your withdrawals and Social Security in the future.

Recently, I met with a couple in their mid-sixties who were concerned about their RMDs (required minimum distributions) down the road. They had heard me rave on the radio show about

Roth accounts and getting out of tax-deferred accounts, but they weren't quite convinced. I ran an RMD Report for them and they were shocked to find out that the $1 million they had saved in their tax-deferred funnel could potentially grow to almost $2 million at an average rate of return of 6 percent by the time they reached age seventy-three, the age when RMDs kick in. At that point, they would have to take just under $80,000 a year as an RMD, which would make a significant difference in how much of their Social Security would be taxed.

Keep Qualified Account		Re-allocate to Tax-Free	
Total taxes paid on RMDs at time of withdrawals	$333,399	Taxes paid on conversion	$250,000
Taxes paid on reinvested RMDs [2]	$116,105	Taxes paid on account growth	$0
Taxes paid on remaining account value at death	$293,775	Taxes paid on remaining account value at death	$0
TOTAL TAXES PAID:	$743,279		$250,000

What options do you have considering that may be your future? For starters, while we're in this low tax environment, if you're in the

12, 22, or 24 percent, in most cases, stop deferring your taxes. Pay your taxes today.

Phantom and Sneaky Taxes

Tax-free investments such as municipal bonds are attractive to some retirees who see them as a way to increase the return on their portfolio. It's true that the gain on such investments will not be subjected to federal income tax, and possibly even state and local tax, but it is still counted toward that Social Security income threshold. The gains on your "tax-free" investment can end up causing you to pay tax on your benefit.

Retirees should also be wary of what is known as "phantom income tax"—money they owe on an investment gain that they never really saw.

A lot of retirees discover that they are paying taxes on income whether they use it or not, even when the market is heading in the wrong direction. That also can be the case for people who buy CDs. Let's say that a person earned $10,000 in CD interest. He is going to get a 1099 showing that entire amount as taxable income. If his investment had been structured differently, he might only have had to pay tax on the amount he was actually using.

Phantom income, therefore, is any income on which you are taxed, that you either did not receive or are not using. For all those retirees whose mutual funds are within their IRAs and 401(k)s, phantom income isn't an issue because the tax is deferred. Instead, they get hit on the back end: instead of paying tax at the long-term capital gains rate, they will be paying it at the rate for ordinary income when the time comes that they have to withdraw their money.

Another hidden tax that people sixty-five and older have to be aware of is something referred to as IRMAA or income-related monthly adjustment amount. The government doesn't call this a tax, but I call it a sneaky tax. It's an income-based premium that you will pay on Medicare if you make more than a certain amount.

For instance, if you are married filing jointly and your income is $206,000 or less, then you will pay the normal Medicare Part B premium, which is currently $174.70. If you are single, you can make up to $103,000 and pay the same rate. After that, however, the premium goes up in increments. For married filing jointly who make over $258,000, the monthly premium jumps to $349.40. A caveat: if you're married filing separately, which the government doesn't like, and your income is over $103,000, then the premium jumps from $174.70 a month to $559.00.

> It is one of those little-known facts about the tax code: if you set up the right kind of program, you can create a tax-free benefit for your loved ones and take tax-free withdrawals for yourself.

With IRMAA, the government looks back at income for the past two years. A one-time exemption can be requested; otherwise, the Medicare payments, which are automatically deducted from Social Security, will continue until you can prove you have a lower income when you file your taxes. I had a client who received a lump sum severance of over $100,000, which put them over the IRMAA amount. When they received the letter informing them of the higher premium, they sent in the forms asking for a one-time exemption and fortunately were approved. But for those who have higher incomes prior to retirement, they're going to pay the higher premiums for at least the first year.

Again, the government doesn't call this a tax, but since it's based on income, what should it be called?

IRMAA can also impact someone's ability to do Roth conversions later. If your income is $100,000, we want to convert as much as possible while the tax rates are low. Or, we may just have to decide that you're going to pay that higher Medicare Part B premium for a while just so we can get as much as possible converted under the lower tax rates.

THREE WAYS TO DISMANTLE THE TAX TIME BOMB

Converting to a Roth IRA

With the rise of Roth IRAs (named for their legislative sponsor, Sen. William Roth of Delaware), qualified investors who meet income restrictions can set up retirement plans in which the withdrawals will not be taxed. Many people approaching retirement, as they assess their financial situation, make the decision to convert their traditional retirement plans into a Roth. They pay the immediate tax owed in order to realize the benefit of tax-free growth and tax-free withdrawals later.

In a traditional IRA, you get a tax deduction when you put the money into the account, so it's considered "before-tax" money. In a Roth IRA, however, there is no deduction: the money you contribute to your investments is "after tax." So, you don't get a tax break when you put the money in; however, if you have owned that Roth IRA for at least five years and you're past age fifty-nine and one-half, then all withdrawals are tax-free. The beauty of the Roth, then, is that it will continue to grow and you will face no tax when you withdraw from it. Nor will there be any tax when your beneficiaries take it out.

In case you're now lamenting that you have a traditional IRA instead of a Roth, it's not too late to pay your deferred taxes and convert. In many cases, it is too late to start contributing to a Roth, if you no longer are working or your income is too high. But there is no income limit preventing you from converting. In some cases, it makes sense to convert the entire account at once, but most often, it's wise to do it over time so you can control the tax hit.

Anyone can convert from a traditional to a Roth IRA. If you have a 401(k) but a Roth is not offered and you're over age fifty-nine and one-half, then you may be able to roll all of your 401(k) into an IRA and then start conversions into a Roth. There are a number of things we have to pay attention to when it comes to converting from a traditional to a Roth. For starters, we don't want you to exceed the top end of the 24 percent bracket with your current income level plus whatever amount we convert. For instance, if you make $100,000 a year and have $1 million in your 401(k) or IRA, we want to convert now while tax rates are low. That means we would have approximately $283,900 we could convert and stay within the 24 percent tax bracket.

For clients considering such a change, we do a comprehensive Roth conversion review, using high-tech software to determine the tax implications and the potential tax savings over your expected lifetime. A lot is involved, such as your age, and whether you need IRA distributions as income, or whether you wish you weren't forced to take them. It depends on the individual or the couple—their needs and what is important to them.

Whether you plan to spend the distributions as income soon is one of the variables that will determine whether it makes sense for you to convert to a Roth IRA. If you are taking money out as income and you're spending down that IRA systematically, then it may not make sense to convert. However, if you're just letting that money pile up to become a big tax burden for your family, then sometimes it makes sense to convert.

We look at other considerations, as well. We know today's tax rates, but we don't know what they will be tomorrow. However, considering the fact that the government is going deeper and deeper in debt every year, it seems obvious that our government has little recourse but to increase taxes. Remember, for much of the last century, the top tax bracket has averaged 61 percent. It's very possible that our loved ones, when they inherit these IRAs, could be in much higher tax brackets than where we are today.

Set Up an IRA Legacy Trust

The IRA Legacy Trust uses a specially designed trust to house a corporately designed life insurance plan. Let's say your IRA distributions each year were $10,000 and you were getting $8,000 of that after taxes. Many people just shuffle that money from their left hand to their right—in other words, it stays right there in their estate. They're not spending it; they're just trying to build the account to leave it to somebody one day, when it will create another wave of taxes.

Instead, you could set up a legacy trust and create a tax-free death benefit. You may be able to leverage that $8,000 per year into somewhere between $600,000 and $1 million of tax-free benefits for your loved ones—a much wiser move than just shifting the money into a mutual fund or CD or other account that will create more tax. A legacy trust not only creates no tax for you, but your heirs pay no tax on the life insurance payout.

A Roth IRA on Steroids

A third way to dismantle the tax time bomb is what we call a Roth IRA on steroids. The goal is to convert an IRA to a non-IRA over a ten-year period, so that you don't create a huge amount of tax burden in any one year. What we do is put that into a "10 pay" (payments for ten years) whole life policy. There are only three that are in existence that work like this. As you put money in, you are leveraging it with a death benefit: you still have your IRA money, but you get a whole life insurance policy, which you may or may not want—it's just an extra benefit.

As you build up a cash value, you can take it out tax-free, while still maintaining that tax-free death benefit. Most of the available plans recently were paying dividends of 6 percent a year or higher, and they are secure against market risk. They have been a great alternative to investing in the market and putting your principal at risk or investing in a CD and earning a pittance.

Let's say you contribute for five years and then decide to pull out $30,000 to buy a car. You can do that, tax-free. The account grows tax-free, you can withdraw from it tax-free, or you can leave it to your beneficiaries' tax-free while leveraging it to a higher amount.

That's why I call it a Roth IRA on steroids. The IRA Legacy Trust uses life insurance benefits really not designed as a cash benefit for the owner. It's designed for a transfer of wealth to the beneficiaries. But in this case, you are using whole life insurance designed to leverage money for beneficiaries, but it's also there for you if you need a tax-free withdrawal. You maintain control over the money, in case you feel you might need it during your lifetime, yet you still leverage the money for your heirs. It gives you the best of both worlds—and is a quite effective way to defuse the tax time bomb.

We also can set up a method for income planning that entails a systematic withdrawal, maximizing income in a way that you know you can't outlive your assets. You spend your money down over your lifetime but know you will not run out, using a hybrid income protection account.

Planning Is Key

When it comes to Roth conversions or other measures to combat the heavy toll that taxes can take, it pays to have a financial planner on your side. We can look at ways to balance your portfolio between the three funnels—taxable, tax-free, and tax-deferred—and begin moving your assets into accounts that pay taxes today when we're seeing some of the lowest rates we're likely to see for years to come.

> **"Planning is bringing the future into the present so that you can do something about it now."**
> **—Alan Lakein**

CHAPTER FOUR

WHAT YOU LEAVE BEHIND

If you want the government to get the biggest share of your estate, you can do nothing and that's what can happen. But with proper planning, you can leave your life's work directly into the hands of your loved ones.

As I mentioned earlier, with or without a will, your estate will go through probate. Though probate isn't the end of the world, it can be a costly nuisance. Probate fees range from around 3 percent up to about 8 percent. If you hire an attorney out of a phone book, it's probably 3 percent, but if it's a family friend, it's probably 8 percent—the ones who know you charge you the most.

A will may only cost $500 to $1,000 to set up. But even if you have a will, it will still go through probate and that could cost your family thousands of dollars later. You may be thinking, "Oh, I've got a will. I'm covered." No. Not having a will means your estate is intestate and a judge has to decide what you would have wanted. But a will won't keep your estate out of probate; it just tells the judge what you want done with your stuff. It's like an engraved invitation, and your family is left holding the bag. Probate can be expensive and time-consuming. There are more effective strategies, as we will discuss, to protect your estate—and your peace of mind.

The Retirement Plan Tax Bomb

In the previous chapter, I talked about the pitfalls of taxes on a retirement plan. Now, let me tell you the story of Bob and Mary, a couple who represent what happens to so many retirees. Bob was never considered wealthy during his working years, but he had done a good job of saving around $300,000 in his 401(k). When he retired, he rolled that over into a traditional IRA account. He and Mary had never planned to tap into that money, and when he turned 70½, he withdrew only the minimum distribution required by law at the time. He did that for years.

Bob died at eighty-three, and Mary, who was a little younger, outlived him by several years. Together, they had taken out a little over $300,000 in required distributions. But they averaged about a 6 percent return on their money, so Mary still had $511,000 in the account when she passed.

Their two children, Bob Jr. and Kathy, each were to get 40 percent of that sum, and two grandchildren, John and Sarah, were each to get 10 percent. The IRA custodian sent out a claim form saying, basically, sign here and this is what you will get. Not fully understanding the consequences, the beneficiaries took the money in a lump sum.

And that's when they found out there was another beneficiary that they hadn't been aware of. His name was Uncle Sam. Uncle Sam's tax take, along with state taxes, was about 40 percent off the top. That meant only $304,000 was left to divide among the heirs.

Bob Jr. and Kathy each got about $121,000, not $205,000. The grandkids each got about $31,000, not $51,000.

Because no planning had been done to change the situation, Uncle Sam became the biggest beneficiary of Bob and Mary's life savings. They bequeathed him over $200,000.

What causes such poor decisions? Sometimes, it's because people just don't know better. Sometimes, it's because people make poor decisions. Sometimes, it's because they're greedy for the money now. Sometimes, it's because of bad advice from advisors who don't specialize in retirement issues and just haven't done their homework.

That's why I try to involve the adult children in their parents' financial coaching, bringing everyone together for a family meeting. I want them to see the best ways to transition the nest egg. We can put provisions in place that work in everyone's best interest—whether they know it or not.

A Mighty Toll

Don't underestimate how much that tax bite could hurt. In estate taxes, for example, a lowering of the exemption from $13.61 million in assets back down to $1 million suddenly puts a great many Americans at tax risk. Most people don't have over $13 million in assets. But many have over a million, once you add up the value of a home, life insurance proceeds, savings, IRAs, and brokerage accounts.

When you're looking at a potential of up to 40 percent federal estate tax on anything above $1 million, that can be significant. A person that has a $1 million life insurance policy added onto their estate could potentially end up giving $400,000 of that back in taxes without proper planning.

Where There's a Will, Perhaps There's a Better Way

It's a fundamental yet critical question: What do I want to leave to whom? How much to family, how much to charities?

A lot of people don't realize what their heirs are going to go through. They want to have enough money for their own lifetimes, and whatever is left, they would like their loved ones to inherit as effectively as possible, but many people just believe that they'd better have a will in place.

Again, if you have a will, your estate will go through probate. If you don't want your loved ones to have to go through the cost and the time of probate, then you need to do some planning besides just drawing up an ordinary will.

It's better to have a normal will in place than to have nothing, because otherwise you can get into all sorts of debate and fighting among family members.

But we have to look at whether there are tax advantages in other planning. The prospect of the $13.61 million exemption from estate taxes reverting to $1 million makes estate planning ever more crucial to an increasingly large number of people. A lot of people—when you add up the value of their life insurance, their IRAs and 401(k)s, their brokerage accounts, their savings and checking accounts and CDs, their home values, and more—exceed an estate value of $1 million. It becomes very important to their loved ones that they do planning that is more in-depth than a simple will.

Even with a $13.61 million estate tax exemption, planning is still important for many people. If that describes you, some simple

> A lot of people don't realize what their heirs are going to go through.

planning can work wonders. If you are married and set up a trust that preserves deductions for both you and your spouse, you could exempt $27.22 million. So much can be done to enhance your contributions to charity. You could provide, say, $1 million in gifts, and by leveraging it with life insurance, you could provide a $3 million tax-free gift to charity.

Setting Up a Trust

If you have more than two children, it is likely that at least one of them has some financial difficulties and trouble handling money. Or perhaps, you have a child who is married to somebody who doesn't handle money well. If you don't want them to get a big chunk of money from your estate, you can use a trust to determine how assets are distributed.

Maybe you only want them to get so much a month or so much a year. Or you could arrange some trigger points, so that at a certain age the child would get a certain percentage, then later an additional percentage, until by the time he reached retirement age, he would have full control. There are a lot of things that can be done based on how you assess the maturity level of your loved ones who will inherit the money. Those whom you believe are irresponsible can have strings attached to their inheritance. It's a matter of what you think is best for the beneficiary. Even from the grave, you'll be able to have a say in how your loved ones are managing your estate and the wealth you amassed over the years.

You also might have children or grandchildren with special needs—perhaps mental or physical disabilities. They may be receiving benefits that they would lose if they received a big inheritance. You can structure a trust in such a way that money will be distributed to them without loss of benefits.

In addition, you may be concerned that a child's marriage isn't stable. If you suspect that divorce is on the horizon and you don't want the money to go out in a lump sum, you can limit how the money is distributed. You can add provisions to the trust that protect the inheritance in cases of divorce—and also from creditors and lawsuits.

Charitable Giving

If your goal is to leave money to charity and the causes you believe in, you can do so in a way that is tax efficient. A good financial coach can lead you in the right direction. You can set up charitable remainder trusts and charitable annuities in which any withdrawals you make during your lifetime are tax-free, and then, the sum goes to the charity. But one of the best ways to leave money to charity is by leveraging it with life insurance.

People often feel they don't need life insurance in retirement, and in many cases, that is correct. They don't "need" it. But it is a means by which we can turn pennies into dollars, so it can be a good leveraging tool if it is used with a purpose. When pennies buy dollars, your life savings do a lot more good than they otherwise would accomplish.

As a retiree, you yourself probably don't need life insurance. But your heirs do. The generations ahead need you to plan in a way to maximize your influence on posterity. If you're purchasing life insurance for a purpose, then it can have great rewards. I know a couple who placed $400,000 in a special income account that is providing a guaranteed $25,000 a year for them, and $18,000

> Through careful estate planning, you maintain control over who benefits from your years of hard work. You decide, not Uncle Sam.

of that is going into a legacy trust. That legacy trust will provide a $2 million tax-free benefit to their heirs. So, what have they done? They have taken $400,000 that they didn't need to use—money that would have become a tax burden for their heirs—and made it produce income. They used most of that income to leverage a huge tax-free inheritance for their loved ones. And they had several thousand dollars left over.

Through such careful estate planning, you maintain control of the money you worked so hard to save all those years. Instead of Uncle Sam's deciding who is going to benefit from your hard work, you choose the beneficiary.

Our planning focuses on what is most important to the client. If a solid income is most important, then we're going to provide the maximum guaranteed income that they could get anywhere.

If leveraging money to loved ones is most important, we'll show how to get the very most for them. If the clients aren't sure which way to go—they want to do something for their heirs, but they're concerned about having enough for themselves—we will try to convert their money into a Roth IRA on steroids. That way, they'll have tax-free income in their future if needed. But it's going to be leveraged into a more substantial amount for their beneficiaries if they don't use it.

Any of those can work. It's just a matter of what is most important to you. If we know what's important, we can help you develop the right strategy to maximize that and to disinherit Uncle Sam—which is the ultimate goal of tax planning.

"It's not the will to win that matters—everyone has that. It's the will to prepare to win that matters."
—Paul "Bear" Bryant

CHAPTER FIVE

IT'S ALL ABOUT TEAMWORK

When I first meet with someone, I strive to understand their goals and passions and how they envision their retirement. I look for any problems that could get in the way of reaching those goals. Once I clearly assess the situation, I set up meetings with a team of professionals with whom I have partnered. Some clients have a great need to consult with a professional in estate planning, for example, or elder law. Some need to see an insurance professional.

Estate planning attorneys help to transfer assets to loved ones while keeping taxes, attorney fees, and probate hassles to a minimum. Elder law attorneys can help a couple deal with the struggles that can ensue if one of them becomes ill. Insurance experts can look at the array of home, medical, and auto coverages and find ways to reduce premiums. Retirement is not a one-size-fits-all proposition. There are so many variables, but the constant is the need for an income that will last a lifetime.

It is indeed all about teamwork. We want to bring together all the assistance that people might need so that they have an organized plan—not just stuff. I recently sat down with a fine couple—he was a retired professor who had a great income, and they had stuff. They had an account with an insurance agent. They had an account with a broker. They had bank accounts and a deferred compensation plan. They'd had a long-term care policy for years. They had an account here and an account there. We talked about everything that they had done, and I'm sure they thought I would congratulate them.

> "You do have some good stuff," I told the couple. "The problem I see here, folks, is that you don't have a plan."

"I have to admit," I told them, "you do have some good stuff. The problem I see here, folks, is that you don't have a plan." I looked at the husband. "Mr. Jones, from what you've told me, if you were to pass away first, your wife would lose 40 percent of your income—and in your case, that's $40,000 a year. How are you going to replace that? What plan do you have in place?"

"I hadn't thought about it," he responded. "I just figured we had enough."

"But do you *know*?" I said. "Do you *know* she'll have enough, and she'll be taken care of, if you back out the driveway tomorrow and get hit by a runaway garbage truck? Is she protected? Do you have a plan in place?"

"Well, I guess not." He looked concerned. His wife looked distraught.

"What our practice does that's different from everybody else," I continued, "is that we take all your stuff and we organize it into a plan—so that you do know. You'll know how your wife will replace your income. She'll know how you would replace hers. If either of you faces a long-term illness, you'll know how to deal with it financially so you can maintain your lifestyle and continue to live life to its fullest."

That couple has the resources to live fearlessly and confidently in retirement. Our philosophy is clear: you must have a plan, and you need a team to help you draft that plan and implement it.

Why the Wait?

Considering its importance, why do so many people fail to plan? Some don't realize the need, or think it's important. Some were so busy working and accumulating—getting their stuff together—that they didn't find the time. Some were oblivious, and some just didn't get around to it.

"Do you love me?" my wife asked me one day.

"Of course I love you," I replied. I knew there was more to come.

"I see what you do for everyone else," she said. "All that talk about planning..."

"Yes..."

"Well, you haven't done any of it for us."

There wasn't much I could say except: "You know, you're right." I was spending countless hours helping others create plans, but I hadn't bothered to put one together for us. Within a few days, we had an appointment with our estate planning attorney and got all our ducks in a row.

> If you fail to plan, then you plan to fail.

The task, for many, can feel daunting, and they often don't realize what they are facing if they fail to plan. They don't realize how much probate can cost their loved ones in time and money and heartache. They don't realize that long-term care is so expensive. They may recall that it costs, say, $2,500 a month for a grandmother, years earlier, and they suppose it's a little more these days. They don't imagine $90,000 a year. And once they understand the expense, they see how their lifestyles would change if one or the other needed such care. A glimpse at the consequences of failing to plan can be a sure cure for procrastination.

Saving for retirement didn't come easily for many. And after forty years or more of hard work, one would hope that those savings couldn't disappear easily either. But they can. As we have seen, just a few bad years can devastate a nest egg that isn't protected. And that realization also startles people into action. They realize the need to be proactive. Whether they were busy or oblivious, the end result is the same: if you fail to plan, then you plan to fail.

But Whom Do You Trust?

It can be hard to know where to go for help. Advice seems to come from all directions—from the newspapers and journals, from radio shows, from the TV talking heads, from folks around the water cooler. It's an information overload. Online, you could spend every waking hour reading financial advice, if you were so inclined. You'll hear one pundit say you should have a will, or you should be investing in the market by all means, or you should be doing this or doing that. Others will insist you need a trust, not a will; or you should pull out of the market, or you should buy bonds and mutual funds. Your head spins: "Will or trust? Take risks or play it safe? What in the world should I do? Who should I listen to?"

And because people aren't sure what to do, they wind up doing nothing. The results can be devastating.

I met several years ago with a couple feeling the pain of procrastination. The husband had Alzheimer's disease, and he had children from a previous marriage. Even though they intermingled their money and spent and saved together, he had never given power of attorney to his second wife. The children from the first marriage showed up on the scene, fretting that she would spend the money that would go to them. They ended up in court, and afterward, she had to give an account of every dime that was spent. It was a real nightmare for this dear lady. Had they just simply put a durable power of attorney for financial assets in place, she could have carried on the family affairs financially just as she had before.

It's such a preventable predicament, and the stress you avoid could add years to your life. Recently, after helping a couple get their financial affairs in order and setting up an income plan that would provide security for both their lifetimes, no matter who died first, they thanked me as we completed their plan.

"Greg, I was having trouble sleeping at night," the husband said. "This is such a relief."

"Yes," his wife added, "we feel so much better knowing things are in order. You brought up things that were worrying us sick. And this takes the pressure off of us."

I hear both kinds of stories from the people who come through my office. "We wish we had only done that," some say. "We're so glad we did that," say others. I so much prefer to hear the latter because I truly love people and care that they succeed.

One of our newer clients is a sweet lady, a widow, who had an advisor before coming to us. She had inherited a few hundred thousand dollars from one of her parents, and the advisor found out about it. She wasn't sure what she was going to do with it because she wasn't sure her advisor was the right fit. She went to his office and he asked her about the inheritance. When she told him she was still unsure, he asked, "Aren't you going to have us help you invest it?" "Probably," she replied, "but I'm not sure yet." At that point, the advisor told her, "Why don't you just go ahead and write us a check and we'll talk about what you want to do." When she told him she did not bring her checkbook to the meeting, he immediately replied, "Yes you did. It's in your purse. I can see it from here." That's how bold some of these people are; it brought tears to my eyes to know that there are people out there who will essentially bully you into working with them. She ended up moving her account to us.

As a retiree, you deserve someone who ultimately has your best interests at heart. The relationship you have with your retirement advisor should make you feel comfortable.

It's time to take the time. You may feel that it's hard enough to plan for a one-week vacation, let alone one that could last thirty years. It can feel overwhelming. But this is certain: if you don't plan, you are virtually certain to be overwhelmed down the road. Stress is probably not what you envisioned for your retirement.

It need not be daunting if you get the right help. You could try to do it all yourself, but unless you are a CPA, attorney, investment wiz, and expert on insurance and taxes all wrapped up in one—and even that would leave you lacking—you are likely to make mistakes, and you are certain to feel stressed out. It's better to delegate. There is so much to consider. You need a team, and you need a coach to bring out the best in you.

Making Beautiful Music Together

A lot of people have tax preparers, and insurance agents, and attorneys. Many elements of their financial affairs are in place but aren't coordinated. Nobody is orchestrating the various aspects so that everything works together.

I have spent many years as a church choir director. The alto section always feels that it is the most important and focuses on its part. The tenor section likewise considers itself the most important, as do the bass and soprano sections. And that's all very typical. My job is to make it all fit together into a beautiful piece of music.

I also find that, when creating a retirement plan, the attorneys think they are most important. So does the CPA and the broker selling financial products. But unless they are working as a team, the plan doesn't come together well. I'm a Los Angeles Lakers fan—and as talented as Kobe Bryant was, it took coach Phil Jackson to get a championship. I'm also an Ohio State Buckeyes fan, and their 2002 national championship was truly a team effort. They were able to put the pieces together.

Someone needs to see the big picture. The players bring plenty of skills to the game, but somebody needs to draw out those talents. That person is the one who can see best where and when to make the plays.

That's where I hope to help the many people who come to see me about their finances. They bring along all their best stuff, but when I learn about their goals, I usually soon see that we need to make it all add up. In our practice, we call it our complete planning review or CPR.

If you already have your own attorney, that's fine. We have a team of professionals, but if you are comfortable with whom you have been working, we will coordinate the efforts. A good retirement coach can work with your current team members. What's important is harmony: you need peace of mind, knowing that somebody is pulling it all together for you. Lack of coordination is a major weakness that I often encounter when I begin the CPR.

I also, at times, encounter people who are reluctant to concede any control over their finances. They seem to feel that by working with a team, they no longer are in charge. Some are do-it-yourselfers who won't give up any control, and I can't do much to help those people. They won't listen. Some tell me they don't want to risk their money, yet their portfolios are heavy with risky investments. They fear they will miss out on a big gain that they are sure is around the corner. They think they have all the answers, yet they're asking for input—or, perhaps, they want validation. In truth, nobody has all the answers. I know I don't. But I do know how to listen to your goals and put together a plan that addresses your needs, concerns, and desires.

Finding Someone to Trust

Those who come to see me are looking for someone to trust, and until they find that person—and that team—they are reluctant to let go of the reins. They want advice and guidance, but they're cautious about who provides it. They are on a mission to find a trustworthy advice giver. It's a matter of building rapport.

I recently worked with a couple who came in with great skepticism. They knew they needed help, but they were far from convinced that we were the right ones to give it. But they needed it desperately. The husband had been managing their investments himself. He had not done horribly, but they had fallen victim to sequence of return risk because they were drawing a monthly income of $2,500 on their investments. He had averaged just under 4 percent over the previous five years, but their account was down by 38 percent.

"Look, folks, I can see your pain," I told them. "I'm here to tell you we can help. Let me tell you about some things that I know we can do for you."

The husband gave me a frank look. "Well, I'm just not sure I'm willing to turn that over right now." His wife interjected that, in truth, they had needed for twenty years to turn over their financial planning to somebody qualified.

"You know, the truth is you can't go it alone," I told them. The rules of the retirement planning game are changing, I explained, and people need to trust the professionals who focus on the financial and legal problems of today. "You won't get the advice you need from a bank teller or your friends."

"It's not as if we haven't done our due diligence," the wife said. "We've done all the things we need to do."

"But there's bound to be more," I explained. "And all those things you've done need to be weighed against one another." I explained that our team included elder law attorneys, estate planning attorneys, and investment advisors, all of whom provide the most complete review available.

"I can see you're worried sick. You don't know whether you will still have enough money. And you don't know if you can trust anyone. But one thing you can know for sure: if it sounds too good to be true, it probably is."

You hear about so many retirees who get talked into poor decisions. Some salesman suggests they can get a phenomenal CD rate that's out of line with any others out there. And everyone and his brother has backyard legal advice. Some get sucked in by online offers; they Google up all these hot tips and have no idea what the source is.

"You're smart, you know, for being so cautious about sizing me up," I told the couple. "You need to know who you're dealing with." It's foolish to hire an advisor without knowing how accomplished he or she is. Good advisors tend to be well known in the community and in the industry. They keep up on things. They're instructors and authors. "And at the end of the day," I said, "you need to trust your feelings."

The wife looked at her husband, and he nodded. Today, they have their affairs in order. Our insurance professional has streamlined their policies. They have a dependable income plan in place. And above all, they have peace. They realized they couldn't do it all. They found someone they could trust, and they let it go.

It's true that there are many people out there who would be happy to sell you a line of goods—or offer advice that is less than sophisticated. You're unlikely to find good retirement planning, for example, down at the bank that you've been going to for the last twenty-five years, the one with the big pillars that services all your accounts. Bank advisors often are in an entry-level position into the financial services industry. They earn little, and most of them are brand spanking new in the arena. Their knowledge is limited. They really only know about the products that the bank sells. There are some notable exceptions, but for the most part, that's what you get at the bank. I know a bank branch manager who told me they have quotas to fill, and failure to meet them brings a reprimand. I would hate to think that my financial plans were based on someone's quota. Yet, that is what can happen if you go to the wrong people who aren't looking out for your best interests.

> You're unlikely to find good retirement planning down at the bank you've been going to for the last twenty-five years.

What to Expect from a Good Planner

It's first things first once you find a qualified retirement planner. We need to work together to get your financial affairs organized so that they line up to accomplish your goals.

First, you need a complete review. Our review process is designed to make sure that nothing slips through the cracks. We consider taxes, healthcare, income needs, and appropriate levels of risk and reward. These all need attention.

We come across people who have spent thousands of dollars in legal fees and produce a big binder filled with trust documents, powers of attorney, and all of the things that are truly valuable tools for retirees. They have those things, but nobody stuck around long enough to help them figure out what needed to be in the trust. We look at the document, and there's nothing in the trust. So guess what? They spent all that money for paper. Nothing was funded or titled in the trust. Nor do they have a clear idea of what should or should not be titled in it.

They feel pretty good about themselves when they show us that binder, but they have no direction at all. "What do you mean?" they say. "Isn't everything all set up?" And I have to tell them that nothing was set up.

There are plenty of people out there willing to sell people stuff. But in my experience, there aren't many who are willing to give them a plan that shows them how to get from A to Z and accomplish their goals as effectively as possible. They need a guide.

I was listening recently to a commercial for a major financial institution. It was geared toward retirement planning, and it touted a product as if it were the answer to your planning needs. And that's the problem. So often, there's no planning involved. It's just sales. Some major institution that everyone recognizes and seems trustworthy says

97

it wants to let you in on a great idea, and that's what is peddled as retirement planning. But a product isn't a plan. It is merely a tool. Unless the advisor took the time to determine whether that tool was appropriate for accomplishing your specific goals—presuming he or she has any idea what your goals are—you are nothing other than a consumer satisfying someone's bottom line. You are advancing somebody else's plan—not your own.

By contrast, we want to see it all. We want to see your tax returns; we want to do a 1040 review and make sure you aren't paying too much in tax. Attorneys make sure that you have the proper documents and that they are up to date. We want to make sure your investments are in the right place to meet your needs and hopes. Are you taking more risk than you thought? We test your portfolio to determine whether or not you need to make adjustments. We consider the income implications if your spouse were to die and whether a plan is in place to replace that income.

It's crucial, therefore, to gather your documents and keep them well organized in a filing system. Where should you keep them? I suggest a fireproof safe at home. A safe deposit box at the bank is a bad idea, because frequently nobody has a current power of attorney to access it. A successor trustee, for example, needs to have a copy of the documentation to prove his status. So, never put valuable papers like that in a safe deposit box. They're better used for things like valuable coin collections that you want to protect from theft. Otherwise, a fireproof safe is best and make sure those who would be handling your affairs know where it is.

After a thorough review of your documents, we let the prospective client know whether we can be of any help. If their goals match their reality, we offer to create a retirement plan. And if it's a go, then we get the team members lined up.

Once the plan is complete, then we start implementing. By then, I tell people, they'll be able to find our office in their sleep. "I'm either going to be your best friend," I say, "or I'm going to be the biggest thorn in your side as we make sure you get all these things in place. I won't let up until we get it all accomplished. I am going to hold you accountable to getting done what you said you want to get done." To be truthful, it can hurt.

Besides reviewing all pertinent papers, we want to learn about the client's goals and priorities. This is crucial, because it's what directs the emphasis in the retirement plan. When I meet with a couple, I spend the better part of an hour asking a series of questions, trying to get them to open up about what is truly important to them. Where do they see themselves in two years, five, ten?

For example, I ask: "What's important to you about money?" I get responses such as "that it be safe" and "that it will last" and "that it's available." I press on: "Available for what?" At first, I may just get *an* answer, but I don't immediately get *the* answer—and that's what I'm looking for, what is truly important to them. That's all that really matters. It doesn't matter what I think. "Well, what do you think?" I often hear, and I tell them that is irrelevant: "It doesn't matter what I think; all that matters is what you care about."

This might be the first time that some of them are really thinking this through deeply. There is an art to drilling down, helping them put into words what they are feeling. Sometimes, couples will sit in my office together and find out for the first time how each has truly felt

> I've seen plenty of tears when couples come to my office for help. Emotions get raw. Husband and wife may have differing expectations.

about an important matter. They'll look at each other in amazement, because they have never verbalized how they were truly feeling inside.

My years of counseling as an assistant pastor really helped me learn to draw things out of people. A wife may be scared to death that her husband is going to gamble away all their savings in the stock market. She has never before opened up and told him about it. In our meeting, the husband might push for some aggressive investment or other, and I'll look at the wife and ask, "How does that make you feel?" And she'll start weeping.

I've seen plenty of tears when couples come to my office for help. We keep a box of Kleenex nearby for when it's needed. Often, it's when couples revisit some disaster that has happened in their life. Or it's when they talk about what they want to do for their children and grandchildren that emotions get raw. Husband and wife may have differing expectations. Even though they love the kids, most don't want them to know how much money they have and what they are planning to do with it.

I often offer to bring family members in, if it seems that would help with continuity in planning. But most are rather private about their finances. We don't typically have the whole family coming in, unless we are dealing with end-of-life issues. In that case, the children may need to know how the finances have been managed and what they need to do to fulfill their parents' expectations. The quality of family relationships can have a lot to do with how a retirement plan is built, and it's during the early talks that those feelings often come tumbling out.

As difficult as this questioning can be, it is indispensable in figuring out what truly matters to the couple. And once I understand that, I look to see where they are financially and the tools they are using in all major categories. "The problem that I see," I say, "is that you are going in about ten different directions. No one has ever been able to show you how to put it together so that it works in harmony. You need to go in one direction. You can do that." And if they want the help of our team, and their goals are realistic, they are on their way to success.

"When you win, nothing hurts."
—Joe Namath

CHAPTER SIX

HERE'S TO YOUR HEALTH

"So, tell me, what's new with you guys?" I asked the couple as we finished one of their regular reviews. For years, I'd been handling part of their retirement planning, but the husband had wanted to take care of most of the details himself. So, I reviewed their investments, we reallocated some of them, and we checked to see that everything was on track. As we parted, I threw out that question to make sure there wasn't some other issue that needed attending.

Big tears welled in the wife's eyes. "We just found out last week," she said, "that he has Alzheimer's." She began to cry.

"Greg, I don't think I'll be able to handle these things myself any longer," the husband said. I felt for them. Many people consider health crises to be something that happens to others, not themselves. Over the years, I'd broached the subject of planning for their health-care, but they had put it off. Immediately, I got on the phone, and soon, we met with our elder law team. It was time for crisis planning.

We couldn't do as much for them as we could have years earlier, but there were still steps we could take to help.

In crisis planning, we use elder law strategies for asset protection. This was a couple with assets that could be lost, and the planning now had to focus on dealing with a healthcare crisis. They hadn't heeded my advice that they needed to attend to this aspect of retirement planning. And now, the husband was facing the loss of the very mental acuity that allowed him to handle most of their financial affairs.

"I'm not doing so bad right yet," he told me. "I'm just in the early stages, but I'm the one who has always handled the finances." He looked at his tearful wife. "She doesn't understand it the way I do."

> Diagnosed with Alzheimer's, the husband was facing the loss of the very mental acuity that allowed him to handle most of their financial affairs.

And so, in crisis mode, we began reorganizing their affairs. Fortunately, he didn't need immediate nursing care. Had that been the case, we would only have been able to spare about half of what they had. The longer he can stay home, and the longer we can employ a series of elder law strategies, the more we can do to protect their assets. We have a plan in place so that we know exactly how we will get them through this.

The week after I met with that couple, I sat down with another couple and learned that the wife had Alzheimer's. Again, we rallied our elder law team. That couple had done some planning for healthcare, but only to a certain point. I've become increasingly adamant about the need to put such matters in place. You've heard the adage that you can lead a horse to water but you can't make it drink. In recent years, when I meet people who won't drink, I've been reluctant to lead them to the water.

In other words, if someone is not willing to make the changes necessary to help protect themselves, there is not much we can do to help.

Many people just don't want to think about getting old, and yet, this is what retirement planning is all about. It's about preparing and making sure you have enough money for the rest of your life. The machinery of our bodies wears out. We age. This is inevitable. We need more doctor visits, more prescriptions, more surgeries.

My dad, after he retired, would say to me, "Greg, everyone said these would be the golden years; they lied to us. Ever since I've retired, I've had nothing but health problems."

Unfortunately, an increasing number of retirees would agree with him. As people live longer, and as medical science is able to keep our machinery going, more people need long-term care—or worry that they will. We need to take good care of our bodies.

You may not be able to run a marathon, and you may not be able to bench-press 300 pounds, but you need to stay active. Staying active can help to keep us youthful, but these bodies do wear out. Physical ailments abound, and dementia and Alzheimer's are on the rise.

As a result, the need for long-term care is on the rise, as well. The average time spent in a facility is about 2½ years, but that doesn't tell the whole story. Many, many people spend only a few weeks or even days in care before they pass on. Others are in a facility for a decade. So, the average isn't typical. It's like the guy who has his head in the freezer and a foot in the oven: "On average," he says, "I'm comfortable."

Married couples, however, should know that the statistics show one or the other of them is likely to need nursing care at some point. The days when older people in need of care would move in with family are over. It seldom happens anymore. Families aren't as close-knit as they once were, and most need two wage earners—leaving little additional time for caregiving. And health needs increasingly require specialized care and you can't get by moving in with the children. Just managing medications can be a complex issue.

Clearly, retirees need to protect themselves financially from the likelihood of needing long-term care. Unless you anticipate and prepare, your life's savings can be ravaged. The expense of long-term care is, indeed, one of life's game changers.

Medicare and Medicaid

Some retirees might feel they could get by with just their coverage through Medicare, for people over sixty-five. However, Medicare pays for skilled facility care only, and it requires a three-day hospital stay. Then, it only pays in full for twenty days. After the twentieth day of skilled care, it pays a portion for a maximum of eighty days. And again, this is only for skilled care, meaning rehabilitation—for example, the care needed after knee replacement surgery. If you don't get better after an extended period, Medicare will take note of that and disqualify the care as skilled. Your care is then classified as intermediate or custodial, for which Medicare pays nothing.

For people who have little in the way of assets, Medicaid can help. In order to qualify for Medicaid, you first must go through a process called spend-down. All your assets except your house, one car, personal belongings, and funeral arrangements are subject to spend-down. A Medicaid counselor would advise a couple to divide their assets, with half under the husband's name and half under the wife's. Then,

> Unless you anticipate and prepare, your life's savings can be ravaged by costs of long-term care.

depending on the state, most of the money must be spent on the care before Medicaid benefits kick in. In Ohio, for example, the institutionalized spouse's half must be spent down to $2,000, and the spouse at home can keep a maximum of $154,140.

At that point, then they would qualify under the asset test for Medicaid benefits. Then, income is considered. The institutionalized spouse must pay all but a small amount of income to the nursing facility. The spouse at home can keep his or her income, up to $3,853.50 maximum.

Spending down assets shouldn't even be on the radar for people who have spent a lifetime acquiring a significant amount of money. A lot of people have done asset protection planning to forestall that possibility. About half of nursing home stays today are paid for through Medicaid. The government is spending billions of dollars a year on nursing home care. Responsible citizens should look for ways to provide for their families without depending on the government.

Though a decision on long-term care should not be delayed, people often don't get around to it. Some have never really thought about it. They haven't slowed down long enough to think about the fact that they are going to get old one day and their health will falter. Some think that Medicare will pay the bill if need be. Others are in denial—"It won't happen to me." Like an ostrich, people put their head in the sand and think everything's fine as danger lurks all around. To those who haven't experienced the issue in their family yet, the odds of needing nursing home care just seem like a statistic.

But doing nothing is not an option, because the consequences can be drastic. In this area of retirement planning, if you fail to plan ahead, you absolutely plan to fail.

Long-Term Care Insurance

Some people consider traditional long-term care insurance too expensive or presume they can't get it because they waited too long. Some do have health issues that preclude such insurance, but others just aren't willing to spend the dollars. Or they may have purchased a policy at the behest of some salesman, but usually it doesn't cover enough. Long-term care currently costs $300 a day, and they have $110-a-day coverage. It's like having a $300,000 house and putting $100,000 of property insurance on it.

A couple should buy at least $300 of coverage per day. They should have a 5 percent compounding inflation rider to keep up with costs in case they don't need the coverage for a few decades. They may never need it, of course. Statistics show that half the population won't need long-term care. Still, if a couple pays $10,000 a year for the coverage for twenty years, they'll have spent $200,000 in premiums. It may feel to them like money wasted.

Long-term care insurance nevertheless can be a good option, particularly if you buy it when you are younger, but be aware that you may not qualify.

Alternative Solutions

Once you have acknowledged that the prospect of long-term care poses a hazard to your nest egg, you can begin to look at a myriad of solutions out there. It is likely that at least one of them will be appropriate for your needs. You should work with someone who can help you match the solution with your goals so that you feel comfortable.

For veterans who served during war time and who meet asset criteria, the Aid and Attendance for Veterans benefit can be a big help in providing nursing care for themselves and their spouses. It won't provide enough to pay for care totally, but it will slow the spend-down process, or it will help to fill in the shortfall for those whose long-term care coverage is inadequate.

And because there is that 50/50 chance your long-term care premiums will go for naught, consider that you might be able to get a plan that would pay out regardless. There are life insurance policies that have special benefits for long-term care. They have been available for several years, and more and more clients are finding it an attractive vehicle.

I sat down recently with a couple, in their late sixties and in good health, who had yet to address their long-term care needs. Like so many, they had been reluctant to pay so much in premiums for coverage that they felt they might never need.

"We can get a $500,000 life insurance policy on each of you," I told them, "that will pay out your death benefit in advance, at 2 percent or $10,000 per month, for long-term care if needed." I explained that to receive the care benefit, they would have to be unable to do two of the following six things: bathing, eating, dressing, continence control, getting into bed or a chair, or managing medication—or else have a cognitive impairment.

"If you want," I continued, "you can pay your own children to provide that care, or a friend, and that could go a long way toward keeping you from ever having to go to a nursing home." It's going to cost the two of you $18,000 a year to have this plan in place, but between the two of you, it is guaranteed to pay out a million dollars. If you live twenty-five more years, you will have paid $450,000 for the protection, and you know the plan will pay out a million dollars, tax-free. It is either going to pay it to you in the form of healthcare benefits, or it will pay to the surviving spouse as a tax-free death benefit, or ultimately, it would go to your heirs as additional funds.

"Either way, this is going to pay off. That 50/50 statistic no longer comes into play. If you need it for healthcare, it pays; if you need care for a terminal illness, it pays; or when you pass away, it pays that tax-free death benefit."

I talked with another couple recently who were in poor health and couldn't qualify for traditional long-term care. He had Agent Orange problems from his days in the military as well as kidney problems and cancer, and she had been burdened with nervousness and depression.

"I'm crazy," the wife told me, "and he's all weirded out on stuff from Vietnam. We can't get anything."

"What if we did some income planning for you?" I asked. She responded that they had all the income they needed.

"Well, you do but you don't," I said. "If one of you passes, you aren't going to have enough income," to which they agreed.

"There is something called a hybrid income annuity," I said, "that rolls up the income base at 8 percent a year. Let's say that for the next ten years you don't need to draw off of that because you have good income now while you both are still living. Then, if one of you dies, this account can be set up to give you $62,000 per year, guaranteed."

"And if you can't perform two of those six activities of daily living, it can double that for up to five years, or $124,000 per year. You don't have to qualify for it with health. We determine the amount of money we need you to put into that account, and you have a plan in place that will replace a lost spouse's income and provide additional money for home care."

For retirees in crisis, we often employ elder law to protect assets. It is within the Medicaid rules to do it, but many people don't know about it.

That couple's long-time broker tried his best to convince

them to talk with him first, but they didn't return his calls. They knew that over the years he had sold them a lot of "stuff" but never put a plan in place for them. Most brokerage houses don't focus exclusively on retirement planning. They don't see the big picture. They work with people on accumulating wealth for retirement, but they don't see how much of a game changer retirement itself is. They lack the knowledge and expertise to help people transition.

For retirees in crisis, as I mentioned earlier, we often employ elder law to protect assets. It structures their finances in such a way that after a certain period of time, those assets are no longer countable toward spend-down. So, someone could qualify for governmental benefits without having to lose a lifetime of savings. It is within the Medicaid rules to do it, but many people don't know about it.

I would rather that people take the other measures instead, but sometimes as a last resort, it is necessary to protect assets in that way. Elder law strategies are there for people who need them. As with the couple who learned the husband had Alzheimer's, the choice is either to lose most of your money or to plan for ways to keep your money.

There are many ways to help protect your assets from a long-term illness, but the most important thing is that you have a plan to address the potential need for long-term care.

"Winners can tell you where they are going, what they plan to do along the way, and who will be sharing the adventure with them."
—Denis Waitley

CONCLUSION

WINNING WAYS

I grew up eating, sleeping, and breathing Ohio State football. I live in Columbus, Ohio, and almost everybody in Columbus loves Ohio State football. In 2000, the team hired Jim Tressel as their coach, and in 2002—when they were picked to be third or fourth in the Big Ten—they went 14-0. It wasn't because they had a lot of great individual players. It was because they had a great team.

They went to the national championship game against the University of Miami, which was on a huge winning streak. The Buckeyes were the underdogs in the game. But with their will to win and their teamwork, they won in double overtime. It was a thrilling, classic victory. You don't become a champion by doing any one thing well; you become a champion by doing all things well.

If you are on a winning team, with all aspects of your financial and retirement planning working together, you are headed toward success. You need that team. A great quarterback cannot succeed if the offensive line doesn't block. A great running back cannot make any yards without that blocking. A great offense can still lose the game without an effective defense.

But with a solid game plan, you stand your best chance of winning. That means having your legal bases covered. That means not letting your money be siphoned away in excessive taxation. That means not subjecting your nest egg to undue market risk or to poor oversight and management. In other words, don't fumble the ball when it matters most. Keep a firm hold on your financial plan.

It's not about how much money you have on the very day that you retire. Rather, it's about what you do with that money. You can have the best intentions of winning, but you need that game plan to give yourself the best opportunities.

Five Core Elements of a Retirement Plan

A successful retirement plan must be complete. It cannot focus solely on investments, and it is much more than simply tax advice. If any of the many considerations that we have discussed in this book are incomplete and exposed to risk, then your entire retirement is exposed to risk. And each aspect must be tailored for your retirement. Yes, you may have an investment plan. But is it a *retirement* investment plan?

Here are the five core elements:

- Retirement investment plan

- Retirement income plan

- Retirement tax plan

- Retirement healthcare plan

- Retirement legacy plan

Try this: Consider each of those elements and grade yourself on a scale of one to twenty points for each, depending on how well you have completed that aspect of your retirement planning. Add up your scores, and how did you fare? A score of twenty in each area would mean you are 100 percent sure of a successful retirement. An eighty means you have an 80 percent chance of success.

Words for the Wise

To enhance that chance and help raise your score, let me offer you six nuggets of advice. If you heed these, you will be well on the way to your own championship season.

Don't go it alone. The rules of the retirement planning game are changing rapidly, and you need trusted professionals who focus on these issues. You won't find them at the counter of your local bank. You won't find them at the coffee shop, beauty salon, or golf course. You need a specialized team with a qualified elder law attorney, registered investment advisor, licensed insurance professionals who specialize in asset protection, and others.

If it sounds too good to be true, it probably is. It's a common and scary trend: retirees ripped off by what they thought was a great opportunity. If you are quoted a rate of return that's far greater than the prevailing one for a product, the red flag should go up. Ask more questions. What strings are attached? If you don't get a straight answer, you most likely should turn and run. There are a lot of great financial products with attractive features, but even the great opportunities out there come with rules and limitations. You need to know what they are and whether they are acceptable to you and in line with your goals. Always trust your own good judgment and common sense.

Beware of legal advice from non-attorneys. We know the value of integrating trust documentation and specific financial products.

However, be very cautious when the purchase of a financial product also entitles you to free legal documents to support the plan. This is where you can be penny wise and fortune foolish. Reliable legal documents cost money, so be skeptical of those that come included as a package if you purchase a product.

Beware of online resources. Today's retirees often jump online to do research about investment products. But ask yourself whether you are getting information from a credible source. Nonsense sometimes masquerades as scholarly advice, and it can be difficult to tell the difference—and even basically sound advice may be the wrong advice for your unique circumstances. Information overload is another problem. If you do an online search for "revocable trust," you will come up with a million or more articles, websites, and resources. Yes, you need to do research, but it should be on the right thing, which is finding the right help. Focus on finding the right planning team to assist you.

Seek out sound advice. When looking for good advisors, assess how accomplished they are. Slick talk can be very persuasive but it may prove financially disastrous. Consider whether the prospect is well known and well regarded in the community and industry. Has he authored anything on the subject? Does she invest in professional knowledge? The answers will show the level of qualifications and passion for the profession.

Be smart and trust your feelings. Credentials are important, but so is your gut feeling. Much is revealed when you meet face to face.

See how you feel. We believe that every person who walks through our office door should be treated like members of our own family. Find a team that fully understands your concerns and priorities and that you can trust. That's what you truly need. You deserve to be treated well.

Hope for the best, plan for the worst. I find it tragic that a person can work thirty or forty years, sacrificing to set aside money for the future, and then suffer a reversal of fortune during retirement, losing half of those dollars because they failed to change strategy. Whether or not it leaves you poor is not the issue. It's devastating to see people's life's work cut in half in just two or three short years. Making sure that you have a plan in place to bring protection and preservation at this stage of your life is absolutely critical. It's important to plan for the utmost in efficiency.

I'm sure Coach Hayes would have agreed. When you throw that pass, the ball could end up firmly in hand for the push to the end zone. Or it could be intercepted. Or somebody could simply drop the ball. The first thing could lead you to the victory. The other two happenings are bad. At this stage of the game, risky investments put you in a precarious position. They may go up, yes. But they may float sideways for years. And they well could fall, perhaps precipitously. It's not the way to win.

When I was a child, my parents taught me to be positive in life and to hope for the best—but not to be foolish. You have to be realistic as well. Plan for the worst. The mistake that most retirees make is to not only hope for the best but to also plan for the best. They keep most of their investments at risk, presuming it will all work out. Often, it does not. If the market stagnates or crashes, their plan fails. The attitude seems to be, "If it's not broke, don't fix it," but it's not a matter of whether it's broken. It's a matter of where you are in life. You see, during the years where your primary goal is to accumulate wealth, the stock market can certainly give you the best opportunity for growth. As you are preparing to transition into retirement, you also have to consider the potential need for income. In retirement planning, we call this a fundamental shift because you are shifting from accumulating wealth for later into distributions to meet your lifestyle needs. Money reacts differently to market fluctuations when you are taking withdrawals than it does when you are just accumulating.

It's a new day, a new economy, and you are in a new phase of life. You need direction. And with direction will come the peace of mind of knowing your lifestyle can be secure for as long as you live. With that confidence, you can pursue your dreams. Do you want to travel? Do you want to spend time with grandkids and help your family? Do you want to be involved in charities and do volunteer work? Perhaps, you want to put an addition on your home, or buy a second home—someplace warmer. If your goals are realistic, and your financial house is in order, you can finally reach for them, free of worry, with a planning team in your corner to keep you on track.

> It's a new day, a new economy, and you are in a new phase of life. You need direction.

In this game of life, it's not he who retires with the most money or the most toys who wins. It's he who accomplishes his purpose, with peace of mind. Money is not an end. It is a means to an end. It allows us to accomplish that which is within us.

Good retirement planning isn't just about reaching for your own dreams, but it's also about your legacy. It's about doing what you feel is right for the generations ahead. Many people feel that what they've done for others while alive is legacy enough, but others want to leave behind something tangible. But whatever we leave, we should leave it behind with purpose—not as a pile of assets for heirs to fuss over.

With some simple planning, we can bring so much more meaning to what we leave behind. We can make it an annual birthday gift to a grandchild. We can make it a foundation that provides for the needy. Alternatively, you can leave money to the attorneys and court systems and perhaps to greedy relatives who may not have cared all that much about you.

Not everybody shares your values and your philosophies, of course, but whoever is giving you advice should surely know those values and philosophies. So, part of your plan should be to make sure that your values are put into action. I have talked to many people who feel their advisors don't really know them. The advisors know how much money they have. They know how much they earned every quarter. But they don't know what's important to their clients. An effective plan is going to capture your values and priorities and advance them throughout your life and beyond.

Who will have control of your destiny? It's impossible to maintain control without planning. You may think you have control and along comes a health crisis. You buy and sell and tend to your portfolio with a keen mind and along comes a diagnosis of Alzheimer's.

Whenever you give up control, somebody or something gains it. A health issue gains control. Or if you suffer a huge loss in the market, Wall Street gains control. You can lose control in a lawsuit. If you pay too much in taxes, the government gains control of that money.

That's the nature of the game changers in your life. If you don't anticipate them and adjust to them and plan for them, they can overwhelm you. But there is no need for that. You have the ability to seize control right now. You can be on your way to a winning retirement.

In Memory of Mary

As I wrote the final chapter of this book, I received the kind of word that all of us dread. A death in the family. Someone very special. Her name was Mary, and she considered me her adopted son.

She and her husband, Jim, had been clients for nearly a decade, and after Jim died in 1999, I would stop by to visit her. I would take her a cream-filled chocolate doughnut, her favorite, and we would sit and talk and laugh and reflect.

After several years, Mary began to struggle with Alzheimer's. Her two sons took her to Georgia to live—and that's where she died, after three years of nursing care. Her sons knew that Mary and I were fond of each other, and they knew about my years as an associate pastor and how I had worked so closely with seniors.

"Would you perform the service?"

The sons stopped by the office afterward. They wanted me to know how much my words of comfort at the funeral had meant to them. But just as comforting, they said, was knowing how much she had gained from her relationship with me—from the warmth of our friendship, indeed, but also from my professional guidance during her retirement years.

No matter what happened, no matter what turns life took during those years, Mary would be all right—and that's something you just have to "know that you know." That's the kind of confidence that brings peace. That's the kind of wisdom that outlasts us.

ABOUT THE AUTHOR

For over thirty years, Greg Taylor, a fiduciary advisor, has been helping people make the right decisions as they launch into what should be the most rewarding years of life. Greg assists retirees and those transitioning into retirement in developing a comprehensive plan so that their savings will last the rest of their lives and beyond, protected from excessive taxes, inflation, and the high costs of healthcare.

Greg and his wife, Kristin, host a weekly radio show on 610WTVN in Columbus, Ohio, and their weekly television show on Sunday morning on ABC.

He is a member of many distinguished industry organizations and has received a national advisor of the year honor for his commitment to client education and perseverance in reaching out to help with retirement planning issues. He has been featured in WallStreetJournal. com, CNBC, Morningstar, Yahoo Finance, MarketWatch, the *Boston Globe*, Forbes.com, and many others. He was listed as one of America's premier financial experts in *USA Today*. He also has appeared on NBS, ABC, CBS, and FOX as a consumer advocate.

In his spare time, he volunteers at his church as part of his passion for missions and ministry. He and his wife, Kristin, enjoy pastimes, including golf, photography, and travel, and hanging out with their three sons.

Legacy Retirement Group, LLC
6315 Emerald Parkway
Dublin, OH 43016
Phone: 614.336.7660
www.legacyretirementgroup.com

IT'S A WHOLE NEW GAME

We've all experienced life's "game changers" that alter our course. We graduate, we marry, we have children, we get that big promotion. And we retire. Happy times—or they should be. But what do you do when those paychecks stop? Suddenly, the rules have changed.

Retirement is a whole new game—and not the kind you find in casinos, though far too many treat it that way. Don't let Wall Street and Uncle Sam steal your joy. Greg Taylor and his team of professionals—experts in elder law, estate planning, insurance, and investments—know how to play it both safe and profitable.

Greg's three-bucket approach can help provide confidence as you transition into one of the most important times in your life. You will have a strategy for liquidity for needs, wants, and emergencies; an income plan to provide what you need to maintain your lifestyle in retirement; and a growth bucket designed to your specific comfort between risk and return.

It takes a good game plan, custom designed for your unique needs, and it takes a dedicated team to lead you to victory. Greg and his team will focus on helping you become more efficient in the five core areas of retirement planning. They want you to be more efficient with risk, income, taxes, healthcare, and whatever you leave behind, having it transition to those you love as efficiently as possible.

Find out more by contacting:

Legacy Retirement Group, LLC

6315 Emerald Parkway | Dublin, Ohio 43016

Phone: 614.336.7660 | Fax: 614.336.7820

www.legacyretirementgroup.com

www.ingramcontent.com/pod-product-compliance
Lightning Source LLC
Jackson TN
JSHW020357141224
75398JS00014B/246/J